Table of Contents

Preface   v

Biographical Sketch of the Authors   vii

Part 1
Background and Introduction   1
to Intercultural Skills

    An Introduction to Intercultural Effectiveness Skills   3
    Carley H. Dodd, Ph.D.

    Overview and Rationale   13
    Frank F. Montalvo, D.S.W.

Part 2
Intercultural Skills for Cognitive   21
and Interpersonal Systems

    Cross-Cultural Psychology as the Scientific Foundation   23
    of Cross-Cultural Training
    Harry C. Triandis, Ph.D.

    Mythology of Life and the Mexican American Experience   45
    Roberto Jimenez, M.D.

    Ethnotherapy: Healing the Wounds of Ethnic Identity   56
    Price Cobbs, M.D.

    Developing Intercultural Self-Worth   65
    Patrick Flores, Archbishop of San Antonio

    Cross-Cultural Reentry   70
    Clyde N. Austin, Ph.D.

Part 3
Intercultural Skills for   83
Corporate Cultural Systems

  A Case Study of a Multicultural City: San Antonio   85
  Henry Cisneros, Ph.D., Mayor of San Antonio

  Multiculturalism and International Trade   92
  Douglas Brannion

  European Consulting: A Perspective on Multiculturalism   99
  Indrei Ratiu

Part 4
Intercultural Skills for   113
Macro-Cultural Systems

  The Media and Multicultural Societies   115
  Samuel Betances, Ph.D.

  The State of Intercultural Education Today   123
  Beulah F. Rohrlich, Ph.D.

  Education Exchange in Europe: Trends and Challenges   133
  for Intercultural Learning
  Roberto Ruffino, Ph.D.

Name Index   146

Subject Index   148

Intercultural Skills
for Multicultural Societies

Editors:

Carley H. Dodd
Frank F. Montalvo

The International Society for Intercultural Education, Training and Research

Washington, DC

Published by SIETAR International (The International Society
for Intercultural Education, Training and Research)
1505 Twenty-Second Street, N.W.
Washington, DC 20037 USA
(202) 296-4710

First Edition

Copyright © 1987 by
Carley H.Dodd and Frank F. Montalvo

Library of Congress Catalog Card Number: 86-62553
ISBN: 0-933934-14-9

Manufactured in the United States of America

10 9 8 7 6 5 4 3 2 1

Preface

From a broad spectrum of professional areas needed in research, counselling, training, management and education, a thread of interest in intercultural behavior is forming a fabric that we choose to call intercultural skills in multicultural societies. A body of multidisciplinary research and practical wisdom that undergirds how to manage intercultural relationships is the focus of this book.

We believed that a volume was needed that distilled the insights of researchers, consultants and practitioners in terms of what it takes to have productive intercultural relationships and functional intercultural systems. Quite naturally, one volume cannot totally address such broad issues. The contributors assembled for this work, however, offer practical observations from their wide intercultural experiences and attempt to summarize key variables, major solutions and significant problems. Each from a unique perspective, the authors in this book describe their framework and each address the fundamental question of intercultural competence.

Some of the authors may be familiar to the reader, others may be new. They were selected by the editorial staff of the International Society for Intercultural Education, Training, and Research (SIETAR International) not only because of their expertise, but also because they represent the society's commitment to improving intercultural relations within and between nations. Many of the articles in the volume deal with state-of-the-art findings, but the book is not intended to be viewed as an annual or to compete with journal articles. However, they clearly present some challenging paradigms, new concepts and solidly based observations that are aimed to cross-fertilize and expand the dialogue among intercultural specialists.

We are deeply indebted to V. Lynn Tyler at Brigham Young University who with his foresights and wisdom brought us together in the summer of 1984 to conceptualize a professional conference and the larger picture represented in this volume. Dr. Michael Prosser originated the idea of a book on intercultural skills, nurtured it and placed priority on its development as president of the International Society for Intercultural Education, Training, and Research (SIETAR International).

However good the planning and ideas, they fade without tremendous effort of an editorial staff. Dr. Diane L. Zeller, SIETAR Executive Director, headed a monumental task of guiding the editorial process of this book. We truly owe Diane the rightful honor of the coming to fruition of the book. Working with her in Washington, D.C. was Jill Christianson, who tirelessly labored to help prepare the copy for publication. Debbie Coon spent tremendous time on this project as Chair of the Publications Committee for SIETAR International.

We also are deeply indebted to our staffs at Abilene Christian University and Our Lady of the Lake University. Special thanks goes to Anna Cloud and to Laura Cates at ACU, and to Josephine Nunñez at Our Lady of the Lake University.

Our chief desire is that this collection be of assistance to intercultural researchers, provide new directions for trainers and practitioners and offer insights to consultants and educators. We look for an ever increasing body of knowledge and research that will add to the fine work done by so many.

C. H. Dodd
F. F. Montalvo

Biographical Sketch of the Authors

Clyde N. Austin, Ph.D., is a researcher and psychologist who has conducted extensive research in cross-cultural reentry stress. The author of two recently published books, he has personally counselled over 600 clients facing reentry stress, including military, federal government personnel, international educators and missionaries. He is a practicing counseling psychologist and a professor of Psychology at Abilene Christian University in Abilene, Texas.

Samuel Betances, Ph.D., is currently Professor of Sociology at Northeastern Illinois University in Chicago. He is host of his own television show, "Inside Out", for the local NBC affiliate in Chicago and a reporter for *Latino Tempo,* which is syndicated to more than 22 cities throughout the U.S. In addition to a varied career, Betances has published extensively on race and ethnic relations.

Douglas Brannion is Canadian Consul-General of the Southwest United States. His experience in overseas assignments is vast, ranging across many years of foreign service.

Henry Cisneros, Ph.D., is a former professor of public policy and political science, and is the present Mayor of San Antonio. He is a successful civic leader and a nationally known political figure. He has served on major national committees on international trade and also is known for this work as a member of the Kissinger Commission in Central America. He is an exponent of intercultural relations and international and economic growth.

Price Cobbs, M.D., is engaged in extensive consulting activities as a psychiatrist. He has conducted a great number of workshops and seminars, is a management consultant, and a well-known author and lecturer. His works include co-authorship of the celebrated book, *Black Rage*. He has investigated ethnic identity among various groups and has an extensive client list.

Carley H. Dodd, Ph.D., is a professor in the Department of Communication, Abilene Christian University. He teaches undergraduate and graduate courses in intercultural communication. His publications include four books and 50 papers and articles on communication. He has served as a consultant with numerous organizations, including Fortune 500 companies and governmental organizations. He is a past Vice-President of SIETAR International and past President of the Kentucky Association for Communication. He lectures widely and has done research in Africa, India, Central America and Papua, New Guinea.

Patrick Flores, Archbishop of San Antonio, grew up in a rural migrant farm family in South Texas. He has become an internationally recognized religious leader in a multicultural community. His work spans numerous years in pastoral care. He has touched thousands, especially in developing insights into the development of positive ethnic identities.

Robert Jimenez, M.D., is a psychiatrist practicing in San Antonio, Texas, whose research and practice has focused on issues in Mexican American identity. He has devoted many years to investigating cultural identity in light of upward mobility.

Frank F. Montalvo, D.S.W., is professor of social work and director of the Intercultural Institute at Our Lady of the Lake University in San Antonio, Texas. His practice, consultation, research, and teaching concerning cross-cultural intervention span over 30 years. He has been on the editorial review board of the *International Journal of Intercultural Relations* since its inception and has published on education and counseling issues regarding cultural minorities.

Indrei Ratiu is an executive with Intercultural Management Associates in Paris, France. He lives in Europe and is engaged in consulting activity with an extensive client list. He has contributed widely to SIETAR International and serves on its Governing Council.

Beulah F. Rohrlich, Ph.D., is a professor of Speech Communications at Syracuse University. Her specialty is Intercultural Communication, which she has taught for 20 years. She has focused a great deal of her effort in pedagogical concerns in intercultural issues and has taught and consulted in many countries. She is past president of SIETAR International and has served in a number of positions of responsibility in professional organizations dedicated to intercultural education.

Roberto Ruffino, Ph.D., lives in Italy where he serves as a trainer, educator, consultant, and researcher in the area of European Youth Exchange. He is the Director of Intercultura and a member of the Board of the American Field Service International Intercultural Programs. He is a past member of the SIETAR International Governing Council and chaired the 9th Annual Conference of SIETAR International in San Gimignano, Italy.

Harry C. Triandis, Ph.D., is a professor of Psychology at the University of Illinois in Champaign, Illinois. A founding member of SIETAR International, he is one of the most eminent scholars in the field of cross cultural psychology. He has authored numerous books, articles, research reports and conference presentations. He is a major editor and is a research consultant.

Part 1

**Background and Introduction
to Intercultural Skills**

An Introduction
to Intercultural
Effectiveness Skills
Carley H. Dodd, Ph.D.

For some time now, specialists in intercultural problems have examined the role of effectiveness in attempting to understand the importance of intercultural encounters. Obviously, as an intercultural communicator, the more effective one can be, the greater the advantages that accrue. Among them are the ability to form better interpersonal relationships, to develop broader economic bases for business, to create more penetrating friendships, to stabilize ethnic identity, and generally to conclude intercultural tasks more efficiently. The social and economic regards of intercultural relationships cannot be enjoyed without an understanding of and skills development in some of the variables surrounding the question of intercultural effectiveness. And, from one theoretical perspective, intercultural effectiveness is an issue cutting across disciplines and across education, training, and research fields.

Some of the parameters of intercultural effectiveness are in fact the subject of the chapters that follow in this volume. Each writer, from some vantage point as an educator, trainer, or researcher, has outlined the kind of variables and the skills that are necessary for optimum functioning in intercultural societies.

In this chapter, however, we choose to engage the reader in pondering some of the recent research on intercultural effectiveness as such. The thesis outlined in this chapter is that several basic assumptions and several fundamental variables contribute to the notion of intercultural effectiveness. In other words, intercultural skills can be understood best by examining background literature into the question of effectiveness.

Assumptions of Intercultural Effectiveness

A number of assumptions need to be mentioned that underscore much of the literature in the area of intercultural effectiveness. Many of these assumptions, in fact, underlie the chapters that follow in this book.

Intercultural Effectiveness is a Skill

Sometimes the skill is cognitive, primarily through a better understanding of a condition or situation under consideration. Sometimes the skill is behavioral, primarily involving a set of actions appropriate for varying conditions in intercultural communication. In any case, one of the assumptions in this book is that intercultural skills produce a condition of intercultural effectiveness. How that skill is applied and understanding the dimensions of what skills are necessary is, of course, the direction of this book.

Intercultural Effectiveness is Desirable

Too many social and economic benefits are lost without adequate attention to the effectiveness and intercultural skills issues. Thibaut and Kelly's (1959) social exchange theory reminds us of the interest most people have in producing the maximum amount of "social reward." Such a statement is not meant to dismiss altruism, but personal motivation behind social relationships can often be attributed to saving face, social advantage or some degree of a self-esteem extension.

Intercultural Effectiveness is Related to a Positive Communication Climate

The point of a communication climate is a significant milestone in the social literature. Gudykunst (1977) identified positive climate and positive outcome as two factors in enhancing effective intercultural contact. Closely akin to the climate notion is the result of research of Gudykunst, Wiseman, and Hammer (1977) where they argue for a third culture perspective, rather that one's own cultural perspective, for producing maximum intercultural communication effectiveness.

Furthermore, the cultural synergy notion advocated by Moran and Harris (1982) indicates that communication climate, or at least creating a non-threatening climate, opens a door for communication, better management, and productive relationships. Several of the articles that follow link effective skills with conditions of ascendancy, inadequacy of communication systems, inept understanding, lack of toleration, and the like.

Intercultural Effectiveness Variables
Can be Identified and Predicted

One thrust of research in intercultural effectiveness is to explore the cognitive variables related to adjustment (and hence to effectiveness) and to define ways to measure those variables. Once they are measured, the user has a predictive profile by which to evaluate a person's skills for intercultural tasks. When deficient, training is provided. In fact, the understanding of intercultural effectiveness deficiency is the fundamental beginning point for intercultural training. The critical question in the process is the nature of the instruments which assess intercultural adaptability and its correlates. A related issue is the nature of the training program to correct the deficiencies, and the delivery system by which to develop adequate intercultural skills. These topics have spawned the development of a growing number of consulting firms dedicated to the goal of assessing and treating problems in intercultural effectiveness.

In addition to these assumptions, let us examine the variables that correlate with intercultural effectiveness. Some of these variables are cognitive orientations, while others are behaviorally oriented. Collectively, though, they represent the boundaries of the state-of-the-art in this field of intercultural effectiveness.

Variables That Predict
Intercultural Effectiveness

A number of researchers have identified correlates of intercultural effectiveness. Some of these studies have focused on task effectiveness, while others have mainly noted intercultural adjustment and stress issues. Our purpose here is to survey the parameters of the variables in that research. For that reason, the predictor variables are presented here without necessarily referring to the full nature of the dependent variables, the sample used, or the length of the study. Nor is this outline intended to define the rank order of these variables, with an exception or two when needed. Rather, the aim, again, is to provide the reader with a backdrop against which to analyze essays in this volume which are context specific, applying the notion of skills to practical conditions.

Insistence on Task Behavior

Research by Ruben and Kealey in Canada and Kenya for two years revealed a number of variables related to cross-cultural

Intercultural Skills for Multicultural Societies

effectiveness (Ruben, 1977). First in order of importance on their list is that insistence on getting the job done can lead to ineffectiveness, at least for skills transfer and development. This role behavior is likely to become even more dysfunctional in cultures where occupational roles and expectations are at odds with cultural norms. If one works for an organization that exhibits an intensive communication style, then one is likely to experience failure within a culture that appreciates a more leisurely pace of work and task behavior. So, developing a cultural fit between one's interpersonal style, one's corporate culture, and the culture in which a person is working is significant.

Self-oriented Behavior

This variable, too, was researched and discussed by Ruben. In their study, Ruben and Kealey found that role behaviors which are self-centered became highly dysfunctional. For instance, they noted that calling attention to oneself, bragging, and showing disinterest in the ideas of the group pretty well spelled disaster for intercultural effectiveness.

Ethnocentrism

The deleterious effects of judgmental attitudes and a feeling of being superior to others from another cultural group are well documented. Ruben (1977) noted that judgmentalness erected barriers to effectiveness. In a series of investigations correlating a scale to measure ethnocentrism (developed by Hood, 1982) with culture stress, Dodd (1985) found a significant correlation, indicating that highly ethnocentric individuals are less likely to adjust well during a transitional experience. Gudykunst and Kim (1984) explained that prejudice and ethnocentrism lead to less effectiveness in intercultural encounters. Furthermore, Tucker and Baier (1982) reported that the ability not to criticize or put down foreigners was significantly linked with intercultural adjustment.

Tolerance for Ambiguity

The ability to react to new but ambiguous situations with little difficulty is a significant skill in intercultural effectiveness. The link between this ability and effectiveness has been established by a number of researchers (Ruben, 1977; Tucker and Baier, 1982; Gudykunst and Kim, 1984; Overseas Diplomacy, 1973; Grove and Torbiorn, 1985).

Empathy

A number of writers explain that the ability to put oneself in the shoes of others is an important relationship skill. But that same ability also links with intercultural effectiveness. To understand things from another's point of view seems critical for a number of circumstances, including communicating innovative ideas (Rogers, 1983) and performing according to one's potential in intercultural communication (Dodd, 1982; Overseas Diplomacy, 1973).

Openness

Observers like DeVito (1983) have noted how a personal stance of openness and flexibility in personal communication style are important for maximum interpersonal relationships to develop and to be maintained. Dogmatism has been significantly correlated with lack of adjustment by linking measures of flexibility with intercultural adjustment and performance (Tucker and Baier, 1982).

Cognitive Complexity

Cognitive complexity refers to the ability of a person to perceive a wide variety of things about another person and to make finer interpersonal discriminations than cognitively simple individuals. Using a sample of Americans working in five countries of South America, Norton (1984) found a significant difference between cognitively complex and cognitively simple individuals such that cognitively complex individuals scored significantly less on measures of culture stress than the cognitively simple individuals in the sample. Gudykunst and Kim (1984) later made the observation that category width, another way to describe cognitive complexity, makes for greater effectiveness.

Interpersonal Comfort

Research also shows that one's ability to feel comfortable interpersonally is significantly correlated with maximum intercultural adjustment (Norton and Dodd, 1984). A similar finding seems evident from other research as well, where interpersonal trust, interpersonal interest, interpersonal harmony (Tucker and Baier, 1982), and interaction (Overseas Diplomacy, 1973) are correlated with effectiveness.

Personal Control

The amount of immediate and personal control one senses about his or her communication environment has been significantly correlated with intercultural effectiveness. Tucker and Baier (1982) found a significant correlation between personal control, intercultural adjustment and performance. Other research also has highlighted significant correlations between personal world view, a kind of fatalism tendency, and cultural adjustment (Dodd, 1985).

Innovativeness

This concept refers to one's ability to try new things, to engage in some social risk taking particularly where new information and developing social relationships are concerned. Evidence suggests that one's ability to try new things is linked with intercultural effectiveness (Overseas Diplomacy, 1973).Roper (1986) reported that innovativeness may facilitate adaptability during transition stress by lowering fatalism and communication apprehension.

Self-esteem

Clearly, one's view of self-worth predicts intercultural effectiveness. A negative self-worth can shake the foundations of one's personal outlook (Bennett, 1977), thus inhibiting effectiveness. Also, self confidence and initiative directly correlate with personal adjustment and performance (Tucker and Baier, 1982; Overseas Diplomacy, 1973).

There are a number of other variables that correlate with intercultural effectiveness that are not listed above, including interpersonal communication and friendships, acculturation motivation, age, occupation, organizational memberships, language competence (Kim, 1977), showing respect for others, interactive skills (Ruben, 1977), positive motivations, positive expectations, trust in people, patience, sense of humor, attitude toward drinking/drugs, family communication (Tucker and Baier, 1982), degree of similarity/difference with host culture, host culture familiarity, and degree of rigidity of host culture (Gudykunst and Kim, 1984). Hammer, Gudykunst, and Wiseman (1978) found three factors that explain communication effectiveness: ability to deal with psychological stress, ability to communicate effectively, and the ability to establish meaningful interpersonal relationships. Researchers and trainers also emphasize the advantages of intercultural training (Grove and Torbiorn, 1985).

Our purpose here is not to be exhaustive of all the variables that contribute to an understanding of intercultural effectiveness, but to provide a background by which to better perceive and evaluate the question of skills. Effectiveness is assumed to be linked as an integral part of the skills development process, and thus, by understanding intercultural effectiveness, we have a clearer knowledge of skills needed in various settings.

A Model for Intercultural Skill Application

In one way, applying the numerous variables listed above to one's personal repertoire of abilities is the clearest approach to developing effectiveness. Obviously, however, a number of climate and situational factors need to be considered. The need is precisely the rationale behind the span of the articles in this volume. Authors from diverse perspectives tackle how intercultural skills function in multicultural societies and consequently illuminate the skills application process.

Another way to look at the research into skills is to pose a model into which these insights may well fit. As the reader can see, the following *Model for Intercultural Skills* explores the factors within intercultural climate systems and consequences:

Intercultural Climate Systems
Cognitive
Interpersonal
Corporate
Macro-cultural
Social
Institutional

⇓

Intercultural Consequences
Skills
Adjustment
Cultural Change
Values and Assumptions
Networks
Goals
Dyadic and Intergroup Relationships

In other words, beyond merely exploring variables that predict intercultural effectiveness, we need to examine the ultimate climates that intervene and affect the ultimate effectiveness outcomes. Those climates include intrapersonal and cognitive frameworks, interpersonal systems, social systems, corporate cultures, and macro-cultures that affect our perceptions, values, and social skills relating to effectiveness.

In the long run, intercultural skills are not "push button" substitutes for understanding. Communication strategies are never mechanistic, artificial ways around loving, warm, personal involvement with people and the hard work to make relationships work. The greatest fabrication of our age may well be that intercultural relationships just exist and demand little attention. There is more than a "pen pal" mentality at stake. The utilization of a skill orientation can make our intercultural relationships smoother, though not necessarily easier at first. In that way, intercultural skills are really the application of an eclectic awareness of factors contributing to effectiveness and a personal motivation to make these work in one's tasks.

Finally, the concepts presented here are a beginning theoretical framework. Some of the concepts are woven into the fabric of the chapters in this book. Dr. Frank Montalvo's chapter that follows lays a functional overview, explaining the correlation among the chapters as they relate to the notion of intercultural skills.

References

Bennett, J. "Transition Shock: Putting Culture Shock in Perspective." *International and Intercultural Communication Annual,* 4. pp. 45-52. 1977.

DeVito, J. *The Interpersonal Communication Book.* 4th ed. New York: Harper and Row. 1986.

Dodd, C. H. *Dynamics of Intercultural Communication.* Dubuque: Wm. C. Brown. 1982.

Dodd, C. H. "A Profile of Variables Correlated With Culture Shock and Personal World View." Unpublished Research. Abilene Christian University, Department of Communication. 1985.

Grove, C. L. and Torbiorn, I. "A New Conceptualization of Intercultural Adjustment and the Goals of Training." *International Journal of Intercultural Relations,* v. 9, n. 2. pp. 205-233. 1985.

Gudykunst, W. B. "Intercultural Contact and Attitude Change: A Review of Literature and Suggestions for Future Research." *International and Intercultural Communication Annual,* 4. pp. 1-16. 1977.

Gudykunst, W. B. and Kim, Y. Y. *Communicating with Strangers: An Approach to Intercultural Communication.* New York: Random House. 1984.

Gudykunst, W. B., Wiseman, R. L. and Hammer, M. R. "Determinants of a Sojourner's Attitudinal Satisfaction." In Brent Ruben (ed.). *Communication Yearbook 1.* New Brunswick, N.J.: Transaction. 1977.

Hammer, M.R., Gudykunst, W.B. and Wiseman, R.L. "Dimensions of Intercultural Effectiveness." *International Journal of Intercultural Relations,* 2. pp. 382-393. 1978.

Hood, Kregg. "Correlation of Ethnocentrism and World View." Abilene Christian University, Department of Communication. 1982. (Unpublished manuscript.)

Moran, R. and Harris, P. *Managing Cultural Synergy.* Houston: Gulf. 1982.

Norton, M. L. "The Effects of Communication Effectiveness and Cognitive Complexity on Culture Shock." M.A. Thesis. Abilene Christian University. 1984.

Norton, M. L. and Dodd, C. H. The Relationship of Self-Report Communication Effectiveness to Culture Shock." Chicago. 1984. (Paper presented to the Speech Communication Association. Nov. 5, 1984).

Overseas Diplomacy. U.S. Navy, Bureau of Naval Personnel. 1973.

Roper, C. "The Effects of Communication Apprehension, World View, Innovativess, and Communication Style on Culture Shock." Unpublished M.A. Thesis. Abilene Christian University, 1986.

Rogers, E. M. *Diffusion of Innovations.* 3rd ed. New York: Free Press. 1983.

Ruben, B. D. "Human Communication and Cross-Cultural Effectiveness." *International and Intercultural Communication Annual*, 4. pp. 95-105. 1977.

Thibaut, J. W. and Kelly, H. H. *The Social Psychology of Groups*. New York: Wiley. 1959.

Tucker, M. F. and Baier, V. E. "Research Background for the Overseas Assignment Inventory." San Antonio. 1985. (Paper presented to SIETAR International Congress, May 15, 1985).

Overview
and Rationale
Frank F. Montalvo, D.S.W.

The other articles in this volume tap the breadth and depth of intercultural experiences and present the skills required for effective management of relationships in multicultural societies. The scope of the volume is not intended to be exhaustive. Rather, it presents the reader with a variety of settings where intercultural competence is essential. All the articles are original and were prepared especially for this volume. They represent state-of-the-art conceptualizations by authors who draw on extensive research and practical experience. The editors encouraged them to go beyond the present state of knowledge by sharing their wisdom, insights, and speculations in order to provide the reader with a vision of the future of intercultural relations.

The first unit in this volume, titled "Intercultural Skills for Cognitive and Interpersonal Systems," discusses the personal, human element in cross-cultural encounters and adjustments as they are experienced by individuals living abroad and within their own country, and when returning home.

Harry Triandis addresses the importance of scientific investigation of cross-cultural training in the lead article, "Cross-Cultural Psychology as the Scientific Foundation of Cross-Cultural Training." The evaluation of how well people are prepared to live and work in different cultures is not only essential for improving their effectiveness abroad, but it provides the basis for conducting professional, ethical training. Trainee satisfaction with their training prior to their intercultural experience is insufficient, according to Triandis. Rather, their post-training adjustment overseas, the host's satisfaction with the trainees and their task behavior must also be measured before the training can be properly evaluated. Among those factors that influence adjustment and satisfaction are the cognitive constructs that provide the trainees with a sense of personal control and understanding of their new cultural environments and that affect their behavior and the host's response. Dr. Triandis enumerates these factors and lucidly discusses a key dimension of cultural difference, the individualist-collectivist continuum. He states that it is the most important contrast between Western and non-western cultures, and an essential conceptual framework for designing cross-cultural training and reducing ethnocentrism.

Triandis' discussion of Hispanic Americans, as an example of collectivist orientation, provides a useful introduction to Roberto Jimenez's article on "The Mythology of Life and the Mexican American Experience." Jimenez is concerned with the radical transition and cultural conflict that many Mexican Americans in the southwestern United States are experiencing. The transition includes a change from semi-rural to urban living; from isolated ethnic conclaves to increased integration in urban areas; from marginal economic livelihood to growing affluence; from blue collar, labor-intensive occupations to information-centered, organizational careers; from a politically dependent status to greater civic responsibility, influence and leadership; and from a relatively isolated, collectivist culture to increased interaction with an individual-oriented society. Jimenez spells out the impact of these changes on the Hispanic's identity and adjustment in terms gleaned from his personal experience and practice as a psychiatrist in San Antonio, Texas. He sees the cultural conflict as an ambivalent struggle by Mexican Americans to change their fundamental outlook on life from their view of men and women as tragic heroes to incorporating the mythology of epic heroism; from struggling to come to terms with one's soul and the good and evil in themselves, and facing death with grace and style to overcoming external adversity rationally and with optimism, industry, and the material symbols of success. This is a basic psychological change that a rapidly changing environment is challenging the Hispanic American's innovativeness. Jimenez provides the reader with an insight into the personal meaning that cultural conflict has for the individuals caught on the crossroad.

Price Cobbs, in his article, "Ethnotherapy: Healing the Wounds of Ethnic Identity," describes the skills needed to understand and help individuals cope with the psychological issues created for ethnic minorities who live in environments where the dominant culture is markedly different. While much of his experience is gained from clinical practice with black and white Americans in the

United States, he views the problems as universal wherever the interacting cultures have unequal status, and individuals feel oppressed and strive to acculturate into the "host" society. The definition of who one is begins on a personal level when an individual first encounters being different from others. For ethnic minorities, this is often defined by parents and peers as belonging to a group that differs from most of the other members of the community, when "we" and "they" are valued unequally. This consciousness of kind creates a tentativeness in interpersonal and intercultural comfort that Cobbs describes as an "eggshell syndrome." It deprives people of open, spontaneous interaction and begins tailoring their multicultural experiences. By withdrawing into themselves and into their own kind, people begin to view society in ethnocentric terms, defining others in terms of their own self-interest. For minorities, the process results in the development of a psychology of the oppressed that burdens them throughout life: a sense of self-doubt, ambivalence and paranoia about interpersonal encounters; reactive aggressiveness geared toward survival in, rather than mastery of, the environment; lack of historical continuity and accomplishment that diminishes pride; a growing feeling of rage that is most often turned inward; and a sense of impotence to control one's own life. Cobbs does not hesitate to draw from his own civil rights experiences in the United States and to encourage the readers to consider their implications on an international scale.

Picking up on the theme of ethnic identity, the Archbishop of San Antonio, Patrick Flores, speaks directly to high school youths in his article titled, "Developing Intercultural Self-Worth." His effort is to help youth accept cultural differences among themselves and to prevent the development of the adult ethnic wounds that Cobbs discussed in his article. His reflections on this serious theme are drawn from around the world and are the personal and often humorous accounts by a person who grew up on rural migrant farms in South Texas in the United States to become a religious leader in a multicultural community. Archbishop Flores is not a professional interculturalist, but his insights into the development of self-esteem and empathy based on his experiences in overcoming cultural differences are as instructive for the reader as they were for the youth he addressed. His presentation was made at an international youth forum during the Congress.

Clyde Austin's article, "State-of-the-Art Research in Cross-Cultural Re-Entry," reviews current research and his international consulting and counselling experience to draw attention to the need for comprehensive scrutiny of the reverse culture shock processes that individuals and families undergo. He focuses on recruitment, selection, training, support, and re-entry as critical stages in evaluation and counselling in the sojourner's international, intercultural cycle. He states that the psychological adjustment problems experienced by individuals returning to their countries are overlooked and worsened by the neglect of parent organizations, relatives and friends. The transition back presents as significant psychological problems for parents and their children as the transition into foreign culture; both represent new sociocultural environments. Lacking consistent cumulative research on the re-entry phenomenon, Austin uses related studies on transitional stress, identity formation and psychology of adolescence to draw parallels with the problems faced by returnees who feel like strangers in their own land. The experience of returning missionaries in the United States and England provides powerful evidence of "cultural dysphoria," a sense of loss and being out of phase with peers, value change and reorientation, and the "embarrassment of riches" and affluence found at "home." He points to specific areas requiring additional research and to the need for improvement in organizations' reception of their returning personnel.

The second unit, titled "Intercultural Skills for Corporate Cultural Systems," presents a series of articles devoted to multiculturalism as a political concept guiding cities and nations in their internal affairs, the growing role of cities in the international business arena, the application of culture-specific information in conducting international business and the need to broaden the scope of intercultural consultation in corporations. This unit begins with two articles by individuals who are not intercultural specialists, but whose professional experience in civic government and foreign affairs provide a broad view of the importance of intercultural communication in conducting successful ventures. The third article, by a human resource development consultant, reviews some major trends in European management that are challenging our conventional approach to training and intercultural consultation.

In the first article, "A Case Situation of a Multicultural City: San Antonio," Mayor Henry Cisneros of San Antonio, Texas, USA, presents the city as a case example of the successful implementation of cultural pluralism in civic life and the city's increased involvement in international business. He speaks, as he says, with a "Texas attitude" of pride in the city's "ethic of intercultural respect" and its visions of the future. The rapid economic growth in the area is accompanied by the inclusion of Hispanic Americans, as the predominant cultural minority group, into the center of political and civic leadership. He alludes, as did Jimenez earlier in this volume, to the city's turbulent social past that has been confronted through understanding and political accommodation and that has enabled the city as a whole to address its economic future. One important road the city is taking is its involvement in international economic cooperation, trade and investments, which are not limited to the city's historically close relationship with Central America. He cites other cities throughout the nation that have assumed leadership in the international business arena. Increasingly, he believes, cities will be concerned with learning different languages and respecting international cultures as they become involved in a global economy. He asks, rhetorically, who is better equipped to help them than those who by training and temperament are prepared to deal with intercultural exchange? To this, we add, who is better to lead these cities than those who view multiculturalism as a resource for growth and development?

Douglas Bannion, as Canadian Consul General in the Southwestern United States, speaks to two themes that parallel those presented by Mayor Cisneros: multiculturalism, but on a broader, national scale, and international trade. Mr. Bannion focuses his discussion of international trade on the interpersonal level by sharing his experiences with companies and their representatives negotiating business across cultures. He provides a practical guide of cross-cultural do's and don'ts for international business visitors to Japan, which is his primary focus. This article is particularly valuable for intercultural trainers because it presents useful intercultural insights gathered from extensive experience in the field.

In "European Consulting: A Perspective on Multiculturalism," Indrei Ratiu presents an overview of the current shifts emerging in human resource development consultation in business and industry that are testing our traditional approach. Organizational productivity and results have become watchwords over concerns for stability, relationships and equity—even among traditional bureaucracies. Organization consultants are challenged to demonstrate the value of cross-cultural communication skills in improving business operations in terms other than improving trust, respect and interpersonal relations. Training, as a strategy to reduce the cost of premature return of overseas personnel, has yet to be proven to European management. He views this as a direct challenge to the cross-cultural training field. Can the belief that cultural difference adversely affects an organization's cohesiveness and effectiveness be proven? Conversely, how can we demonstrate that cultural diversity contributes to an organization's innovative and flexible capacity? Why are some corporate mergers culturally compatible and others are not? These are but a few of the questions raised by him that underscore his view that the traditional Organizational Development approach is too limited in scope to address the new issues emerging in European intercultural consultation. Ratiu calls for a re-address of our knowledge base to include broader conceptual frameworks that answer questions about corporate cultural change, adaptablilty and compatibility.

The third unit of this volume views intercultural skills from its broadest base, education. The role of the public media in structuring our beliefs about intercultural experiences is analyzed by the first article; the second reviews the historical development, objectives and current state of intercultural education; and the traditional view of the purpose of educational youth exchange programs is called into question by the third.

In "The Media and Multicultural Societies," Samuel Betances discusses the media's powerful impact in the United States on the development of identity among women and cultural minorities, and the importance of intercultural specialists to approach their consultative work with passionate commitment for bettering the lives of their clients. He draws on his experience as an international consultant on cultural issues affecting developing nations to focus the reader's attention on the subtle influence that the media play in negating cultural differences and limiting the country's full use of its human resources. Commercial radio, television and films have the potential of enlightening the public to the multicultural reality of life in the United States and abroad, and to end the divisiveness that they create out of ignorance and misinformation. He urges the professional in the intercultural field to regard the media as potent forces in multicultural societies and to use his or her knowledge and skills to shape their influence. Betances' statements add to the views discussed earlier by Jimenez and Cobbs regarding ethnic identity, and to Rohrlich's discussion of intercultural education in this section.

Beulah F. Rohrlich's review of "The State of Intercultural Education Today" is described as climbing a mountain without any trails, an attempt to put in perspective a field of practice that lacks coherent theory, terminology and traditional framework. Yet, she succeeds in ordering the state of knowledge and methods used in teaching intercultural communication. The article is marked by her cogent evaluation of the current literature in the field, her analysis of key concepts in common use, and the guidelines she provides teachers in designing courses on multiculturalism. Rohrlich recognizes the strong influence that the mass media have on intercultural understanding and recommends its positive use in the classroom with specific examples.

Roberto Ruffino believes that the potential intercultural value that student exchange programs can provide is unrealized because they are not appreciated, understood, and designed properly. In "Educational Exchange in Europe: Trends and Challenges for Intercultural Learning," he comprehensively traces the history of educational exchange programs and the self-serving philosophical and pragmatic use to which some of them were put. These were counter-productive to their intent to improve international understanding. With clarity and insight from many years of experience, Ruffino states the proper goals of exchange programs to include improved knowledge of self, readiness to love, and an acceptance of ambiguity. He traces, for the first time in print, the major trends and motives in youth exchange programs over the past 40 years. In the process, he delineates the administrative problems, political and methodological issues and the obstacles affecting each trend. It is appropriate that this volume ends with Ruffino's comments on the importance of people-to-people programs in Africa that pull together the international strings of intercultural peace, development, change and identity.

Part 2

**Intercultural Skills for Cognitive
and Interpersonal Systems**

Cross-Cultural Psychology as the Scientific Foundation of Cross-Cultural Training

Harry C. Triandis, Ph.D.

In my view, cross-cultural training is now where medicine was in the 19th Century. It provides a service, the clients are satisfied and pay; but there is serious doubt about the validity of much of what is being offered. That was the way medicine was in the 19th century. My grandfather was a physician in the northern part of the island of Corfu, in Greece, and he practiced not only in the 19th century, but also the first third of this century. His practice, as best as I can determine from talking to him when I was a child, and to my mother who often helped him, consisted largely of giving placebos. He argued that most of the illnesses of his clients were psychological and what they needed most was to be reassured. A placebo does just that. Besides, he argued, his clients could not afford the expense of much medicine, and when they were *really* sick he sent them to the hospital in town, where they got sophisticated treatment. I must add that he was beloved by his clients, and when he died they mourned him for months. So, by just delivering mostly placebos and telling people something comforting, he did what by the standards of his time was not a bad job.

If you compare that performance with modern medicine, there is a vast difference. Modern medicine with its scientific basis, its double blind tests, and emphasis on surgery, can make a *real* change in somebody's life.

My thesis is simple: what physiology is to medicine, crosscultural psychology is to cross-cultural training. It is important to establish much stronger links between what you do and the scientific work that is relevant to what you do.

The essence of science is self-correction. Scientists are engaged in a perpetual conversation with nature, which very often suggests that they are wrong. That is very important. Only by finding out that one is wrong can one improve performance. One must constantly expose one's ideas to a test; furthermore, one must have ideas that are vulnerable and thus can be modified. This way knowledge accumulates. If cross-cultural training is to become a profession, like medicine is today, it must move in that direction. To do this one needs to link much more clearly with cross-cultural psychology.

Introduction

What is Cross-cultural Psychology?

It is the study of the behavior and experience of individuals whose background includes at least two cultures. Culture, for this discussion, may be defined as an aggregate of individuals who can communicate because they share language, time and place. In other words, they are individuals who live in the same environment, at about the same time and share a language. It is the *sharing* that is an essential element of culture. It may be the sharing of unstated assumptions, beliefs, norms, values or behavior patterns. It is this sharing that results in coordinated action and increases the chances of survival.

Criteria of Cross-cultural Training

The criteria of successful cross-cultural training must include: (a) how satisfied, or well adjusted, is the trainee in his new cultural environment, (b) how satisfied are the hosts with the trainee, and (c) is the task that the trainee or the hosts or both have set for themselves getting done?

Clearly, if the trainee experiences intense culture shock, or the hosts expel him, or tasks that the trainee or his hosts set for themselves do not get done, cross-cultural training has failed. Ideally, an evaluation of the effectiveness of training would use all three of these criteria; however, if you have clear evidence that your training makes a difference on even *one* of them, it is better than nothing. In all honesty, how many of the training programs that you have used has been tested this way? I fear, that unfortunately, the answer is very few. I urge you to correct this and to seriously consider validation of the training you provide. Evaluation of such training is complex, and multifaceted (Triandis, 1977), but it can be done. I urge you to establish such evaluation as the essential standard of your work.

Factors That Influence These Criteria

Of course, research so far has not provided definitive information about the factors that influence, much less determine, the three criteria. Nevertheless, there is a vast body of information that is relevant, some of it cross-cultural. I will touch on some of it.

Loss of control and culture shock. There is a vast amount of evidence (see Langer, 1983) that humans feel depressed when they are unable to control what happens in their environment. Such lack of control can be traced to several factors. The behaviors of the trainees in the new culture do not get rewarded at the usual rates, either because their habits are inappropriate or because they do not understand what leads to what. Or, they feel upset by novel stimuli, or do not know the norms and roles that require specific behaviors. Each of these determinants of behavior (Triandis, 1980) can be traced to culture to some extent. Culture is in part a set of schedules of reinforcement (Skinner, 1953) and shapes habits and behavior patterns. What is functional in one culture is dysfunctional in another. Our task is to analyze precisely what behaviors must be extinguished and what new behaviors to put in their place. Some of these are obvious and easy to identify, as, for instance hand shaking in the West versus bowing in the East. Other behavior patterns are far more subtle and difficult to identify and teach. Teaching about norms and roles is also in part easy and in part too subtle and difficult. It is easy to specify "when you are in a tea ceremony and someone passes you the cup you are supposed to offer it back." It is much more difficult to teach someone that if tea is served with a banana that means that something is not matching properly. Obviously in the latter case one needs to know enough about frequencies to detect that tea and banana is an infrequent pairing, and hence that it has a special meaning.

Exposing the trainee to the sounds, smells, tastes, and tactual experiences of the new culture, as well as the behavior patterns that are common in that culture, can help increase liking for them. Zajonc (1968) has shown that mere exposure to a stimulus increases liking for it. But the trainer must select those stimuli that are both frequent in the new culture and infrequent in the trainee's culture.

A lot of the behavior that the trainee will encounter in the new culture is interpretable correctly only if the trainee knows its causes. This is why I have argued that it is important to teach the attributions that people make in different cultures (Triandis, 1975). If we can make sure that the trainee makes attributions about behavior in the other culture which are isomorphic to the attributions made by members of that culture, that increases the similarity in the meaning of behavior perceived by the trainee and the members of that culture. The culture assimilator's main function is to do that.

In addition, the trainees must see their culture in relation to the other culture on a number of key dimensions of contrast. That will allow them to have a *cognitive framework* for interpreting what they see in the new environment. I have suggested (Triandis, 1984) a cognitive framework that can be used by anyone going to another culture to sort out the multiple observations s/he is bound to make there. Knowing that cultures differ on some dimension increases the chances that relevant behavior will be noted, remembered, *and* understood.

Meeting the expectations of the hosts. There is very little, if any, research on what maximizes the good impression of the hosts. In all probability a trainee who is more or less like the hosts in attitudes, beliefs, norms, roles, and values and behavior would be a big hit. But, clearly, this is a tall order. If we had to make our trainees perfect bilinguals, with complete mastery of the two cultures that would be great, but it is economically unattainable. So, the research issue must be restated: What can we sacrifice and still result in hosts who are satisfied with our trainees? My guess is that *language* is the most important element, but it also is the one that is most time consuming to acquire. The second most important may be sufficient sensitivity to the host's subjective culture (attitudes, beliefs, categorizations of experience, norms, roles, and values) to allow the trainee to avoid offending with inappropriate evaluations of events occurring in the host's culture. In such a task the trainee would be greatly helped by broad rather than narrow categories (Detweiler, 1980), and by low levels of ethnocentrism (i.e., using own culture as a standard for judging the other culture).

Getting the task done. Here we have a vast literature on organizational and industrial psychology which has relevance to task performance. It has been reviewed elsewhere (Tannenbaum, 1980). The key point I want to make is that cultural dimensions interact with a lot of what we know about organizational behavior (Triandis, 1982). Thus, again, if we have a set of dimensions that can sensitize the trainee, we can increase the chances of the task getting done.

Summary of the Argument to This Point

To provide training that will maximize the three criteria mentioned above it would be most helpful to identify some of the major dimensions that contrast cultures. Cross-cultural psychology focuses on the relationships between ecology, culture, and behavior. Ecology and culture shape what individuals perceive, and many of their cognitive processes. Such cognitions are associated with various affective states. Perceptions, cognitions, and affect determine the person's behavior. That behavior is a major factor in the person's adjustment to the host culture, in the reactions of the hosts and in the accomplishment of the tasks. Thus, identifying the mechanisms that link the above mentioned variables to each other is essential for the understanding of how to obtain the best results on the three criteria presented earlier.

Psychology vs. Cross-cultural Psychology

The links between experience and perception, cognition, and affect are studied by psychologists. The contribution of cross-cultural psychology is that it examines how cultural variables interact with such links. In other words, while a phenomenon may be universal, there are variations of the phenomenon that are culture-bound. Culture often modifies relationships among variables. Similarly, perceptions, cognitions, and affect determine behavior, but the links are again influenced by culture. So, the task of cross-cultural psychology is to spell out how culture acts as a parameter of psychological theories. A parameter, according to the dictionary, is "a constant whose values determine the operation or characteristics of a system". So, the analogy is that particular relationships may take one form in one culture and a different form in another culture. If we know the level of a parameter, we know which form the relationships will take.

Analyzing Culture

To use culture as a parameter we need a set of dimensions that can contrast cultures. I have presented such a set of dimensions elsewhere (Triandis, 1984) and it would be repetitive to present them again. Each of these dimensions needs to be studied intensively, with multimethod methodologies and methods that are culturally sensitive. That is, with methods that allow the point of view of the hosts to become salient.

Ideally, we need to show that observations, interviews, questionnaires, surveys, content analyses, and ethnographies converge and indicate that some cultures are high and some other cultures low in each dimension. In addition to behavioral patterns that correspond to each dimension, we should probe the kinds of *categorizations* used by members of the culture, the kinds of *associations* among categories, the *beliefs, attitudes* and values of members of each culture, their *norms* and *roles,* and the way they relate to other groups, including their *stereotypes, likes and dislikes* for other groups, and *social distance* from other groups. These observations and measurements must co-vary in order to establish a dimension. As an illustration of such work, I will outline my work on the dimension of individualism-collectivism.

Individualism-Collectivism

First, it is useful to distinguish individualism vs. collectivism, at the level of cultures, from idiocentric vs. allocentric orientations, at the level of individuals. The observations that one makes at the psychological level ought to indicate that in each culture there are individuals who are allocentric as well as individuals who are idiocentric. When we sum across individuals and correlate data across cultures, that is with the number of cultures as the number of independent observations, we find a pattern similar of individualistic or collectivist responses. That kind of analysis allows us to see how the beliefs, attitudes, and values of allocentrics in an individualistic culture are similar or different from the beliefs, attitudes, and values of allocentrics in collectivist cultures, and we can also study the corresponding data for idiocentrics. In other words, I am not arguing that cultures are monolithically collectivist or individualist, but that some dominant patterns along these dimensions can be detected.

In my view, the individualist-collectivist dimension is probably the most important contrast between cultures, because it reflects aspects of the evolution of cultures. For about 99 percent of the time that humans have been on the face of this earth, they survived by hunting and gathering. That activity took two forms, depending on how effective each form was in the particular ecology: it was done in groups or in a solitary manner. If one can be more successful by working alone, as occurs in a territory that has very few animals (e.g., the Eskimo), one tends to do the job alone or in pairs; if one can get more done as a group, one does it that way (e.g., cooperation to dam a river, poison the water with poisonous leaves to paralyze the fish, and to catch the fish). Most of the hunting-gathering people who have survived to this day live in isolated parts of the globe (the Arctic or deserts) where the first type of hunting is successful. So, Berry (1976) has shown that these people tend to emphasize self-reliance and independence when they raise their children, and that makes them protoindividualists.

Agriculture started just yesterday, in geological time, and required more cooperation. Clearly, an irrigation system cannot be developed by a single person. Thus, collective action was emphasized. Berry (1976) has shown that cultures that emphasize cooperation also emphasize obedience to authorities who direct the collective action, and raise their children to be obedient and dependent on authorities. So, collectivism emerged.

The industrial revolution has occurred a mere moment ago, in geological time. It has created immense wealth for some people. Such wealth has made it possible for them to become independent of their ingroup. Thus, neoindividualism emerged.

If we neglect the preliterate societies of the world, we have societies that have moved from the dominance of agriculture to the dominance of industrial society in different degrees and in different historic periods. England moved into an industrial society first. Historians are still debating whether English individualism emerged at that time or had already been an attribute of that culture by the 14th Century. One historian has argued that individualism in England developed because of the system of primogeniture—the eldest son getting all the land and the others having to make a life of their own, thus becoming independent of the group, having to be self-reliant, etc. I do not think that is a good explanation, since primogeniture, I understand, has been a pattern in China and Japan also. I suspect that the emergence of individualism requires a favorable ratio of resources to population. If one *can* be independent, one becomes independent. Industrialization increases resources, as does a frontier (and of course, the prototype of the individualist is the participant in the opening of the American West in the 19th Century), as does a city (which is often associated with higher levels of wealth), as does migration (which usually moves people to regions where the resources to population ratio is more favorable).

Whatever the causes of individualism, there is a good deal of evidence that it is a major contrast between cultures. First, take the

Hofstede study (1980). Using a sample of 117,000 people from 50+ countries, summing the responses of the subjects in each country, and factor analyzing across countries, he found that Power Distance accounts for most of the variance and Collectivism was his third dimension. But in most of the data, the correlation between Power Distance and Collectivism was very high (around .7). So we are dealing here with a huge amount of the variance accounted for.

Most sociological and anthropological systems of values have identified the contrast between individualism and collectivism. For example, Parsons, Kluckhohn and Strodtbeck, and others have made it one of the dimensions of their systems. In a study by Mezei (1974), which examined the responses of American undergraduates to the Kluckhohn-Strodtbeck values, individualism-collectivism was the factor that accounted for most of the variance.

Now exactly what is collectivism?

Harry Hui, who is from Hong Kong and took his doctorate with me, did his dissertation on this subject. He wrote to 81 of my social science acquaintances around the world and sent them a questionnaire and asked them to indicate how, in their opinion, would an individualist and a collectivist answer those questions. To make a long story short, the 46 psychologists and anthropologists who answered, and more than half of them were not Americans, showed a good deal of convergence in their answers. The themes that emerged were the following:

Collectivists tend to:

1. give more consideration to the implications of their own behavior for others, than do individualists,

2. share material and non-material resources with others more than individualists,

3. be more willing to agree with others in order to avoid a fight,

4. feel more shame than guilt when they break a norm,

5. share outcomes (both good and bad) with others, and

6. feel part of other people's life more than do individualists.

On the basis of these ideas, Hui constructed a questionnaire in both Chinese and English, which tapped how people relate to parents, kin, neighbors, friends, and co-workers with respect to such themes.

He found that the items formed reliable scales, and that individuals were more or less collectivist with respect to parents, kin, neighbors, friends and co-workers. Illinois undergraduates were more collectivist than Hong Kong undergraduates on the parent and neighbor scales; Hong Kong undergraduates were more collectivist on the friend and co-worker scales than were the Illinois undergraduates.

This, he argued, made sense because the Hong Kong students had to be more emancipated from their parents than most young people of their age group in order to go to that particular university and stay in its dormitories (where they were tested) and neighbors are generally a nuisance in Hong Kong, and there are a lot of conflicts among them. However, friends and co-workers are responded to in a much more interdependent manner than he had noticed in the U.S.

He validated his scales by showing convergent validity with other scales (e.g., the Interpersonal Orientation Scale of Swap & Rubin, 1983 and the Social Interest Scale of Crandall, 1980); validities were in the .2 to .5 range, depending on the collectivism scale.

He also showed that one can predict specific judgments that people make about social dilemmas on the basis of their answers to these scales. For example, "Suppose," he asked his subjects, "you are playing a game of frisbee with a friend and your friend breaks the neighbor's window. How much of the cost of replacing the window should you contribute?" The answers were such that both a percent of contribution to the neighbor and to the friend could be obtained and these percentages were highly correlated with the corresponding neighbor and friend collectivism scales, but the correlations were quite specific, i.e., you cannot use the friend collectivism scale to predict how much of the neighbor's costs a person is willing to cover.

On the basis of Hui's studies we can identify both some collectivist and some individualist themes, which are shown in Table 1.

Table 1

Themes Suggested by Hui's Study

Collectivist Themes	Individualist Themes
Obtain parent approval before deciding on who to marry.	Decide who to marry independently of parent's approval.
Borrow and lend appliances from a friend.	Make sure you are self-sufficient with respect to all needed appliances, so you neither borrow nor lend to friends.
Take time off from your busy schedule to help a friend who needs your help.	Not disrupt one's busy schedule to help a friend who needs help.
Agree with your good friend's views about religion or politics, so you do not have a fight about such topics.	Argue with your good friend, if you disagree about religion or politics, even if that results in a fight.
Worry that your friend may find out if you did something that you feel ashamed about.	Not worry that your friend may find out if you did something that you feel ashamed about.
Feel ashamed if you find that your good friend hit his wife in the course of an argument.	If your good friend hit his wife in the course of an argument, it would not result in your feeling ashamed.
Feel honored when your close friend wins a national award.	When your close friend wins a national award, you feel glad but it would be wrong to say that you "feel honored."

U.S. Hispanics are more collectivist than non-Hispanics. In Table 2, I listed some of the ways in which this shows up.

Table 2

Hispanics are more Collectivist than Non-Hispanics

Evidence:

Hispanics are more likely to spontaneously mention that they would miss their families, if they were to join the Navy; also they show greater concern with meeting their family obligations (Triandis, 1981). Intensive family attachment shows also in anthropological observations (Rojas, 1981).

Hispanics express avoidance of interpersonal competition (Triandis, Ottati and Marin, 1982).

Hispanics emphasize being sensitive, *simpatico*, loyal, respected, dutiful, gracious and conforming; nonHispanics honest, conservative and moderate (Triandis, Kaskima, Lisansky & Marin, 1982).

Hispanics emphasize personal cooperation and interpersonal dependence (Ross et al., 1982).

Hispanics more willing to make sacrifices in order to attend family celebrations (Triandis, Marin, Betancourt, Lisansky & Chang, 1982a), but this tendency is reduced with acculturation (Triandis, Marin, Betancourt & Chang, 1982).

Hispanics emphasize the high probability of positive and the low probability of negative social behaviors relative to nonHispanics (Triandis, Marin, Betancourt, Lisansky & Chang, 1982b).

Hispanics find it difficult to distinguish a person from a role (Rojas, 1982) and experience a strong pull toward their families (Triandis, Marin, Hui, Lisansky & Ottati, 1982) while work groups are viewed ambivalently (Large ingroup/outgroup distinction).

One of the most interesting aspects of that set of data concerns the so called *simpatia* script. A cultural script is a culturally unique pattern of behavior. The Hispanics show this pattern. Namely, they show a strong tendency to see higher probabilities of positive events and lower probabilities of negative events in social behaviors.

Here are some examples of the questionnaires we used: the role differential (see Table 1) and the antecedent/consequent method (see Table 2) provide examples of the kinds of judgments we asked Hispanics and nonHispanics to make. We then computed the means for the Hispanic and the nonHispanic samples. We found a strong tendency for the Hispanic means to be higher in the case of positive social behaviors and lower in the case of negative social behaviors. For example, Table 3 shows a summary of these data.

Table 3

Number of Times the Mainstream Means are Higher or Lower than the Hispanic Means. (Number of times the difference between the means is statistically significant in parenthesis).

	Hispanic Means Higher than Mainstream	Mainstream Means Higher than Hispanics	z-value	p-value
ALL SUBJECTS				
Positive Behaviors	20 (3)	8 (0)	2.6	.005
Negative Behaviors	2 (0)	25 (12)	4.2	.000

One can also break down the data by level of acculturation (See Table 4). Again the *simpatia* script is present, but more strongly in the case of the less acculturated than in the case of the more acculturated.

Table 4

	Hispanic Means Higher than Mainstream	Mainstream Means Higher than Hispanics	z-value	p-value	Mainstream	Hispanic	t-test	Probability
SUBJECTS WHO HAVE BEEN IN THE U.S. FOR A SHORT TIME								
Positive Behaviors	21 (7)	7 (0)	3.1	.001	.63	.71	-2.51	.01
Negative Behaviors	2 (0)	25 (15)	4.2	.000	.17	.09	4.82	.000
SUBJECTS WHO HAVE BEEN IN THE U.S. FOR A LONG TIME								
Positive Behaviors	10 (0)	18 (0)	-1.6	.5	.63	.61	.42	NS
Negative Behaviors	3 (0)	24 (3)	3.8	.000	.17	.13	2.22	.03
SUBJECTS WHO ARE EXPOSED MOSTLY TO SPANISH MASS MEDIA								
Positive Behaviors	17 (5)	11 (0)	1.1	.12	.63	.67	-1.23	.2
Negative Behaviors	4 (0)	23 (8)	3.4	.000	.17	.12	2.99	.004
SUBJECTS EXPOSED MOSTLY TO ENGLISH SPEAKING MASS MEDIA								
Positive Behaviors	18 (0)	10 (0)	1.6	.05	.63	.64	-.43	NS
Negative Behaviors	1 (0)	26 (9)	4.6	.000	.17	.10	3.82	.000
SUBJECTS WHOSE ATTITUDE IS NEUTRAL TOWARD ENGLISH SPEAKING CO-WORKERS								
Positive Behaviors	18 (4)	10 (0)	1.6	.05	.63	.65	-.8	NS
Negative Behaviors	2 (0)	25 (9)	4.2	.000	.17	.11	3.67	.000
SUBJECTS WHOSE ATTITUDE IS POSITIVE TOWARD ENGLISH SPEAKING CO-WORKERS								
Positive Behaviors	20 (2)	8 (0)	2.6	.005	.63	.66	-.97	NS
Negative Behaviors	2 (0)	25 (6)	4.2	.000	.17	.11	2.99	.004
SUBJECTS WHO HAVE HAD NO ENGLISH SPEAKING FRIENDS OR ROMANTIC PARTNERS								
Positive Behaviors	20 (3)	8 (0)	2.6	.005	.63	.67	-.118	NS
Negative Behaviors	2 (0)	25 (12)	4.2	.000	.17	.11	3.42	.001
SUBJECTS WHO HAVE HAD ENGLISH SPEAKING FRIENDS AND ROMANTIC PARTNERS								
Positive Behaviors	17 (2)	11 (0)	1.1	.12	.63	.65	-.52	NS
Negative Behaviors	6 (0)	21 (6)	2.7	.004	.17	.11	3.29	.002

This, then, indicates that one of the elements of collectivism, as identified in Hui's study, the desire for harmony, the tendency to agree in order to avoid a fight, takes a special form among Hispanics. They try to be *simpatico*, charming, likeable. To do so they emit more positive social behaviors and avoid negative social behaviors. Confrontation is used only as a last resort.

We also collected data with a questionnaire, and we summed the responses to such questions and found, after factor analysis, three factors: Subordination of Own Goals to Other's Goals, Extension of Self onto Others, and Concern for Others.

We also identified allocentrics and idiocentrics, with Hui's questionnaire and then examined how these samples answer a variety of scales. We found that allocentrics are less anomic and alienated, and idiocentrics are more lonely. The quantity as well as the quality of social support received is higher among allocentrics than idiocentrics, and the two samples had distinct value emphases: the allocentrics valued most cooperation, equality and honesty; the idiocentrics valued most a comfortable life, competition, pleasure and social recognition (see also Table 5).

These are preliminary findings. We are now in the midst of collecting Japanese data and more will be available shortly. The major point I want to make here is that one can subject this dimension of collectivism-individualism to empirical research.

Given what we have learned so far, how can we define individualism and collectivism and what theoretical considerations should guide future research?

Lewin (1951) presented a theory which argued that behavior is determined by the person and the environment as it is perceived by the person. He called this the psychological field of the *life-space*. So, individualism is the case where the ingroup (family, tribe, friends, co-workers, depending on the person and the culture) is at the center of the life space. That means that if one changes ingroups, one is an entirely different person. That can explain the behavior of Japanese prisoners during the Second World War. They were instructed to fight to death. Those who did not discovered that their captors treated them decently. So, when one of them offered to guide the American bombers over Japanese territory, the American military asked anthropologist Benedict: "Can we trust him?" and she

Table 5

Allocentric Subjects	*Idiocentric Subjects*
Emphasize concern for different ingroups*	Little concern for ingroups
Emphasize harmony in interpersonal relations within ingroup**	Confrontation, competition are acceptable within ingroup
Distribute rewards according to equality or need***	Equity
Are attracted to those who use equality very strongly***	Slightly
Emphasize group goals	Individual goals
Low in anomie	High in anomie
Low in alienation	High in alienation
Do not feel alone	Feel alone—loneliness
Feel part of stable social system—long term goals	Feel temporary allegiance and short term goals
Group based on what maximizes group effectiveness	Group sensitive to cognitive similarity
Perceive that they receive more social support	Homogeneity of ingroups makes them susceptible to group think, but also more innovation
Perceive that they receive better quality of social support	Are higher in achievement motivation
Value cooperation, equality	Value comfortable life, competition, honesty pleasure, and social recognition

Note: Results contrast US subjects high and low on allocentrism, with the exception of the items that have a star which come from other studies as follows:

      * Hui (1984)—Hong Kong Chinese and US Illinois Ss.

      ** has been found in Hong Kong as well as in US studies comparing Hispanics and nonHispanics.

      *** has been found by Leung (1983) in studies of Hong Kong Chinese and US Illinois Ss.

said "Yes" and subsequent events proved her correct (Hall, 1969). How can we explain this? Our theoretical perspective suggests the answer. They had changed ingroups, so they were different people.

In individualistic societies, people have many ingroups and they enter them easily and leave them when the rewards for participation in the group are smaller than the costs. In collectivist cultures people have few ingroups and they are so strongly dependent on them that they do not leave them even when the reward/cost ratios are unfavorable. Loyalty is a great virtue.

In individualistic cultures, ingroups determine a narrow segment of social behavior. In collectivist cultures, the ingroup's influence on social behavior is broad and diffuse, as well as deep.

Thus, in collectivist cultures, individuals are constantly focused on the ingroup: the needs, attitudes, and values; the goals of the others guide their own attitude, values and goals. In individualist cultures, it is the individual's goals that matter. The ingroup is *used* by the individual, if the ingroup can provide enough rewards to overcome the costs of the association with it, one stays in the ingroup. Furthermore, the individualist has a short time perspective for relating to ingroups: if the reward/cost ratio drops below unity, for a short time, he simply changes ingroup. In fact, in many cases the individualist will form new ingroups that suit him better.

As a consequence, in individualist cultures, people work mostly on individual tasks and take responsibility for the success or failure of these activities; in collectivist cultures, the group is the unit of analysis (Nakane, 1970). Tasks are given to groups and the groups are responsible for success or failure.

Future Research

We are currently developing culture-sensitive and appropriate methods for the measurement of allocentric tendencies in many cultures. After that is done we hope to be able to study whether allocentrics are the same or different when we study them in individualistic or collectivistic cultures. We also will check if the results we have obtained so far can be replicated. Table 5 lists the results we have obtained to date.

Next, we plan to study if individualism is associated with other dimensions of cultural differences. Table 6 shows some of the hypotheses that seem worth testing. It could be that individualism is associated with field independence, universalistic communication (Glenn, 1981), pragmatism, low power distance, internal control of motivation, loose normative control (since there are numerous ingroups that may have contradictory norms) and a particular set of behavioral patterns. Conversely, collectivism may be associated with field dependence, associative communication (where only ingroup members understand what one is talking about), ideologism (since ingroups have monolithic ideologies that permit agreement on ideology), high power distance, external control of motivation, tight normative control, and a different pattern of emphases on behavior.

Note that if these hypotheses are supported, we will have a very powerful conceptual framework for thinking about social behavior across cultures. Such a conceptual system could be taught to people who interact with members of cultures that differ from their own in the several dimensions of collectivism and individualism we are discovering.

It should be clear that identifying the network of relationships outlined above will provide a broad conceptual framework for cross-cultural training.

Table 6:
Hypotheses for Future Research
PATTERNS OF CULTURAL DIFFERENCES

Individualism	**Collectivism**
Many ingroups	One or two ingroups
Small attachment to ingroups	Strong attachment to ingroups
Ingroup/Outgroup differences small	Ingroup/Outgroup differences large
Create own ingroups	"Natural ingroups"
Own goals take precedence over ingroup goals	Own and ingroup goals indistinguishable or ingroup goals take precedence
Confrontation is used	Harmony is stressed
Individual tasks	Group tasks

Possible Correlates (to be investigated)

Field Independence	Field Dependence
Universalistic communication	Associative communication
Pragmatism	Ideologism

Low Power Distance	**High Power Distance**
Authorities are consultative, voting	Authorities are paternalistic
Status differences are rejected	Status differences are accepted
Age is not a positive attribute attribute	Age is a positive attribute
Status is achieved	Status is ascribed

Internal Control	External Control
Self-concept: competent, powerful, active	Self-concept: weak, passive
Value: doing, being-in-becoming, dominance over nature	Value: being; subjugation to nature; supernatural
Loose Normative Control	**Tight Normative Control**
Emotional control not important	Emotional control important
Tolerance for ambiguity	Intolerance for ambiguity
Multiplicity of norms, norm conflict is high	Clarity and consistency of norms

Dominant Behavior Patterns

Emphasis on individual achievement performance assertiveness material success	Emphasis on group achievement performance Pride in lifestyle
Aggression is O.K. both in ingroup and with outgroup members	Harmony with nature
	Interpersonal support highly valued
Independence is valued	Interdependence highly valued
	Within ingroup aggression is taboo; aggression to outgroup is quite acceptable.

References

Berry, J. W. *Human Ecology and Cognitive Style*. New York: Wiley. 1976.

Crandall, J. E. "Adler's Concept of Social Interest: Theory, Measurement and Implications for Adjustment." *Journal of Personality and Social Psychology, 39*. pp. 481-495. 1980.

Detweiler, R. "Intercultural Interaction and the Categorization Process." *International Journal of Intercultural Relations, 4*. pp. 275-293. 1980.

Glenn, E. S. *Man and Mankind: Conflict and Communication Between Cultures*. Norwood, NJ: Ablex. 1981.

Hall, E. T. Statement at the Hearings before the Committee on Foreign Relations, United States Senate, 91st Congress. Washington, DC: Government Printing Office, p. 15. 1969.

Hofstede, G. *Culture's Consequences*. Beverly Hills, CA: Sage Publications. 1980.

Langer, E. J. *The Psychology of Control*. Beverly Hills, CA: Sage Publications. 1983.

Lewin, K. *Field Theory in Social Science* New York: Harper. 1951.

Mezei, L. "Factorial Validity of the Kluckhohn and Strodbeck Value Orientation Scale." *Journal of Social Psychology, 92*. pp. 145-146. 1974.

Nakane, C. *Japanese Society*. Berkeley: University of California Press. 1970.

Rojas, L. *An Anthropologist Examines the Navy's Recruiting Process* (Tech. Rep. ONR-4). Champaign, IL: University of Illinois, Department of Psychology. 1981.

Rojas, L. *Salient Mainstream and Hispanic Values in a Navy Training Environment* (Tech. Rep. ONR-22). Champaign, IL: University of Illinois, Department of Psychology. 1982.

Ross, W., Triandis, H. C., Chang, R., & Marin, G. *Work Values of Hispanics and Mainstream Navy Recruits* (Tech. Rep. ONR-8). Champaign, IL: University of Illinois, Department of Psychology. 1982.

Skinner, B. F. *Science and Human Behavior.* New York: Macmillan. 1953.

Swap, W. C., & Rubin, J. Z. "Measurement of Interpersonal Orientation." *Journal of Personality and Social Psychology, 44.* pp. 208-219. 1983.

Tannenbaum, A. S. "Organizational Psychology." H. C. Triandis & R. Brislin (Eds.), *Handbook of Cross-Cultural Psychology*, v. 5. Boston: Allyn & Bacon. 1980.

Triandis, H. C. "Culture Training, Cognitive Complexity, and Interpersonal Attitudes." R. Brislin, S. Bochner, & W. Lonner (Eds.) *Cross Cultural Perspectives on Learning.* Beverly Hills, CA: Sage. pp. 39-77. 1975.

Triandis, H. C. "Theoretical Framework for Evaluation of Cross-cultural Training Effectiveness." *International Journal of Intercultural Relations, 1.* pp. 19-45. 1977.

Triandis, H. C. "Values, Attitudes and Interpersonal Behavior." *Nebraska Symposium on Motivation, 1979.* v. 27. H. Howe & M. Page (Eds.). Lincoln, NE: Nebraska University Press. pp. 195-260. 1980.

Triandis, H. C. *Hispanic Concerns About the U.S. Navy* (Tech. Rep. No. 1) Champaign, IL: University of Illinois, Department of Psychology. 1981.

Triandis, H. C. "Dimensions of Cultural Variations as Parameters of Organizational Theories." *International Studies of Management and Organization, 12.* pp. 139-169. 1982/83.

Triandis, H. C. "A Theoretical Framework for the More Efficient Construction of Culture Assimilators." *International Journal of Intercultural Relations, 8.* pp. 301-330. 1984.

Triandis, H. C., Kashima, Y., Lisansky, J., & Marin, G. *Self-concepts and Values among Hispanic and Mainstream Navy Recruits* (Tech. Rep. ONR-7). Champaign, IL: University of Illinois, Department of Psychology. 1982.

Triandis, H. C., Marin, G., Betancourt, H., & Chang, B. *Acculturation, Biculturalism and Familism among Hispanic and Mainstream Navy Recruits* (Tech. Rep. ONR-15). Champaign, IL: University of Illinois, Department of Psychology. 1982.

Triandis, H. C., Marin, G., Betancourt, H., Lisansky, J., & Chang, B. *Dimensions of Familism Among Hispanic and Mainstream Navy Recruits* (Tech. Rep. ONR-14). Champaign, IL: University of Illinois, Department of Psychology. 1982a.

Triandis, H. C., Marin G., Betancourt, H., Lisansky, J., & Chang B. *Simpatia as a Cultural Script of Hispanics* (Tech. Rep. ONR-19). Champaign, IL: University of Illinois, Department of Psychology. 1982b.

Triandis, H. C., Marin, G., Hui, C. H., Lisansky, J., & Ottati, V. *Role Perceptions of Hispanic and Mainstream Navy Recruits* (Tech. Rep. ONR-24). Champaign, IL: University of Illinois, Department of Psychology. 1982.

Triandis, H. C., Ottati, V., & Marin, G. *Achievement Motives of Hispanic and Mainstream Navy Recruits* (Tech. Rep. ONR-5). Champaign, IL: University of Illinois, Department of Psychology. 1982.

Zajonc, R. "Attitudinal Effects of Mere Exposure." *Journal of Personality and Social Psychology Monograph Supplement, 9.* pp. 2-27. 1968.

Mythology of Life and the Mexican American Identity*

Roberto Jimenez, M.D.

This chapter explores the Mexican American experience in the Southwest, at least as we have seen it and felt it in Texas, particularly in the San Antonio area. There are some differences in New Mexico, Colorado, and California, but I think there are more similarities than differences, and San Antonio exemplifies the rapid cultural transition perhaps more than any other Hispanic community in the Southwest.

Cultural Transition

We are at a period of crucial transition, a period of radical transformation, of culture conflict, of loss and change. Readers with sociological and psychosocial backgrounds are very familiar with what happens to societies caught in a state of culture conflict, and the kind of issues and problems that begin to evolve in such a situation. This chapter touches on that evolution, some of the symbols, and some of the mythology that we are beginning to retrieve—that vital thread of continuity. How can we integrate the experiences, values, customs, and material goals of our forefathers with new cultural experiences, mobility, and relationships? Let us look at the evidence in terms of this crucial transition in which the Mexican American now finds himself. This transition parallels the Irish, Greek, Italian, Chinese, Jewish, and Rumanian immigration experiences in some respects; in others it does not.

The literature suggests we are in a period of incredibly rapid change. The pace is alarming, but there are some peculiarities in the changes that are taking place in our nation and the entire industrialized West. This change is now not only quantitative but it is also qualitative. We are being thrown into experiences that the world has never even seen before.

For instance, the nuclear age and the computer age have given us new forms of organizing ourselves for doing business that we have had no prior experience with. There is this element of discontinuity and its negative effects. In the bereavement literature, people suffer and die in terms of unresolved grief reactions when they lose loved ones, lose a job, lose a country, or lose a culture. If there is a radical upheaval in a nation, like in Cambodia or Laos, of the homeland, and no way of ever going back, then it seems dead. Consequently, it becomes exceedingly difficult to have some sort of continuity from the past as you move into the future. This continuous change causes major problems. The kind of experience that we are struggling with in our nation is becoming more and more this type of change.

For instance, look at the curriculum in our public schools. History is considered irrelevant. I remember growing up in San Antonio, and recall how the history teachers had a lot of prestige as they told the parallels of the Roman Empire to our current society; they also told about the previous experiences of peoples around the world and how we could learn from that. However, such status rarely exists today

Urbanization

Our nation's people have gone from a rural to an urban society within the span of 40 to 50 years. Incredibly, sixty-five percent of the people in our nation just at the turn of the century lived in rural and semi-rural areas. Now, seventy percent live in cities, semi-urban areas or suburbs of cities. That is a very short span of time for an entire population to make such a shift. Within the Mexican American group we were lagging 10 to 30 years behind others. We just made that shift after the Second World War and mostly after the Korean War, after the 1950's. We were still a rural, semi-rural people until the mid-1960's. Now eighty percent of us reside in cities and that is even a shorter span of time for us to make a rather radical transition. An important connection here is the impact of the non-human environment on personality formation, and the little literature available describes the negative impact of changing geography, changing surroundings, and embracing new surroundings where one has very little experience; in this case, large metropolitan areas.

For the Puerto Ricans that came to New York, thousands of them were working in the sugar cane fields in Puerto Rico; literally overnight they were dumped into Philadelphia and Boston, having to live in high-rises and ghettos with absolutely no experience with plumbing, with electricity, with the hazards of living in tall buildings. I recall, for example, in the Boston City Hospital, having to fight with social workers because they would call the cops on the Puerto Ricans for neglect and child abuse because their kids would come in with burns and fractures. They were falling out of windows, they were getting run over by cars, and these mothers were "not taking care of these children." They did not know how. They never had to worry about that kind of experience before. When they lived in villages with buildings on the ground with no high windows, surrounded by neighbors and family, the kids would jump out of the window and everyone would take care of them. They never got hurt, and all of a sudden they are living in a ten or fifteen story apartment building not geared for children. It will take a generation to get these folks acclimated to a place like that. Yet they had to do it literally overnight; so of course, the psychosocial consequences have been immense. The results of the rural to urban transition need significant study.

Physical Labor to Sedentary Work

We went from a physically active labor to the type of work that we call sedentary, where we tend to utilize the higher part of the center of the brain more than our backs and our arms, and that was also a radical transition. We had not done that kind of work before. It is not that we are incapable of it. I think we've demonstrated very well that we're as capable of cerebral activities as our non-Hispanic brothers and sisters. But we never had an opportunity in this nation to prepare for a service-oriented, information-centered environment. That's primarily a post-Vietnam War era phenomenon.

From Isolation to Interconnected Culture

We also went at an alarming rate from being a relatively isolated culture to a culture that is not interconnected. Ten years, fifteen, twenty years ago no Mexican American could get elected to anything, not even to dogcatcher. San Antonio, for instance, was still run by non-Mexican Americans, even though we were the majority for twenty years, and it was a segregated city; we did not go beyond Main Street into the downtown area. If we did, there would be fights and we would be hurt; then when we got home we would get hurt again because our fathers after beating us would say, "What business do you have there?" We had our own stores, our own schools, our own churches, our own radio stations, our own food, our own language and our own neighborhoods. There was no need for us to relate to the outside world and vice versa. Now we can't do that. The mainstream culture now likes tacos and enchiladas, although they would not eat "that trash" fifteen years ago. Now, of course, people are making fortunes. Again in San Antonio, the Mexican American millionaires of today are people who owned restaurants, tortilla factories, and so forth. They could barely make a living selling food to other Mexican Americans, because nobody would pay those kinds of prices for tortillas and enchiladas.

As we went from an isolated to an interconnected culture, we have been thrown into having to mix and relate to others and to cope with the consequences. We came from a society that was self-sufficient, where we didn't need any input from the outside world. We had our own economy, and we had our own juvenile delinquency problems; no social workers were needed. We probably were not doing a very good job, but we did it anyway. It was kept in-house. Now we have to depend on schools and social services, and the economy of the city, banks and credit cards.

What does all this mean? It means that we have had to learn very quickly the way of doing business in an urban area that relies heavily on cerebral activity where you have to deal with and depend on all kinds of people from different races and cultures. You have no choice for your survival but to interact whether you like it or not.

Personal to Impersonal Identity

Now we have to move from a personal to an impersonal identity. In South Texas, in Puerto Rico, in Cuba or the Dominican Republic, if you meet another Hispanic from the previous generation for the first time, the instinctive questions are: "Where are you from? Do you know so and so? Do you know this family?"

This personal relationship is how we orient ourselves. What clan do you belong to and what territory are you from? And then we make conclusions about people from Albuquerque that they are nice, they pay their debts, they do not kill you and stab you, they've got very nice ways down there, they greet you and whatever. You judge others from the kind of families they come from; whether you can trust them or not. If you go to Boston or New York or San Antonio and observe this kind of experience in the non-Hispanic community, one of the first questions that a non-Hispanic, non-Black is interested in is "What do you do?" What kind of job, what sort of career do you have? In the mainstream culture, the sociologists have demonstrated that occupation is the biggest orientation force in personality formation in the modern technical, industrial state, not family and not roots. The evidence is quite impressive in terms of the role of occupations in identity formation.

A similar condition is happening to women now entering the work force. Their struggles are with the transitional identities as mothers and life givers to corporate, medical, and engineering leaders. The change in those roles leads to psychological, psychosomatic, and stress issues involving women. This phenomenon for the non-Hispanic, though begun over half a century ago, is accelerating now. But for the Mexican American, for the Hispanic in general, the transition is happening literally overnight. So the impact is enormous.

This generation is experiencing a cultural communication gap, most visibly seen in interaction with their parents. For instance, they do not know the family language anymore, nor are they interested in learning it. They are bored with it. They do not understand why their parents simply do not buy them anything they want, and the parents are just as confused. In roller coaster fashion, parents will splurge for the children one week and cut them off the next. The lack of experience with all this new-found money leaves them no way of modulating themselves. So the disasters are unreal.

The Impact of Transition:
The Struggle of Myths

What is the nature of this impact? What is this culture conflict ripping the Mexican American apart at the very inner sanctum of the soul? He does not want to talk about it, but to understand it; look at his literature, poetry, and his dance. An irony of a festival, for instance, is that you can feel the joy and the sadness simultaneously. The young Mexican American in his soul is often unaware of this feeling. My experiences as a practicing psychiatrist, a student of human behavior, and from counselling with upwardly mobile Mexican American and Hispanic professional types (as well as adolescents from previously poor families turned wealthy) exposes a fundamental struggle of outlook. What is this struggle?

Epic Versus Tragic Myths

As I see it, we have the struggle of new fundamental outlooks or myths of life: the struggle between the epic and the tragic sense of life. Anglo American culture, Teutonic culture, and Anglo Saxon, too, were inherited by England and imported into the United States; these still pervade in a sort of mythology of the Anglo American experience. Although there have been other elements put into it, by and large those have dominance. The American culture includes a number of aspects: the Protestant Reformation with its accompanying Calvinistic work ethic and philosophical precepts, the scientific revolution, the Enlightenment in regard to rationalism, and the importance of the higher cortex centers in resolving their issues and problems were the main ingredients. If you want to get a feel for the heartbeat of this culture, this Anglo American culture, look at the literature, the music, the dance, the sort of unconscious experiences and expressions of this mythology.

Consider the story of Beowulf where a monster raided the village and killed the children. The people's hope, after years of endurance, stemmed from a myth that a blond, blue eyed youngster would be born and save them from this prophecy. The people were expected to study the stars and history, and find clues in order to identify this young blue eyed hero. They also had to fashion a sword with superfine steel that only that youngster could use. They had to train and nurture him so he could be provided an opportunity to slay this monster. They found the boy, trained and raised him, and fashioned the sword. When he was of age and with a little luck, with a little help from his friends, with some ingenuity, he went out, found the monster and killed the monster. He got rid of the evil forever and the people lived happily ever after.

The moral of the story is to discover problems and conquer them. Life is a struggle between good and evil, and man is basically good. Consequently, if you want to live happily, you tackle problems with Yankee ingenuity, have a little luck and the right technology, but you have to study the problems before resolving them.

In one sense, then, mainstream culture involves an epic people. Franklin Roosevelt was able to garner the strength of Americans at one of the worst periods in American history, the Great Depression, when there was gloom and pessimism. He stated, "America has a rendezvous with destiny." The very epic statement is contained here:

the problem can be resolved. You just have to get the right solutions by involving the brightest thinkers.

But what about a tragic people? Hispanic Culture is a culture that stems from a mixture of pre-Columbian civilizations and the culture that was imported from Spain in the 14th century. It is a culture that stems from the Counter-Reformation, the Spanish Renaissance. The Spanish Renaissance was the period of growth in Spain and Portugal after the defeat of the Moslems during the abolition of the Arabic people in the Hispanic areas of Europe. Spain and Portugal were feeling fortunate. God had given them that victory and the Pope declared them defenders of the faith and gave them a mandate to spread the faith and guard it from the Protestants who were threatening to destroy it. The anti-Christ was introducing evil things such as science and industry, machines, happiness, money, etc. Spain entrenched itself in a very defensive posture and a counter-Reformation movement spread the Catholic gospel, as Spain understood it, to the New World by the sword. They had learned from the Arabs and other earlier cultures. They got their best minds to produce philosophical defenses against the Protestant onslaught. One of the most creative periods in Hispanic History occurred, namely: the poetry, literature, and theology. The Hispanics were developing a way of life. They went after peoples' souls.

The Hispanic culture is one that emphasizes the "within" of things. The conquest is not the outside world, but the inner world: one's soul, and the conquering of death. This is the big issue in our Spanish culture and all our rites and rituals symbolize it.

For example, in the old days bullfighting was a way of life, and the bullfighter would die in the ring. If he were only disabled in the ring and could no longer fight, then he would have to learn to cope with the loss and the change or commit suicide. The idea of bullfighting is that a man faces the bull, which represents life and the inevitability of death. The bullfighter knows that at some point the bull will be victorious. It could be today; it could be tomorrow. But ultimately the bull will win the struggle. The bullfighter will be gored, killed, or disabled. But he dresses up. He dances out and stares the bull in the face and says to him, "I know that someday you will kill me. It could be today, it could be tomorrow. I know that, and I'm going to show you what it's like to kill a man, but between now and then you will wish that you had never taken me on." Then the ritual starts. It is a dance. The problems identified with the bull and the bullfighter are enmeshed in this mythology as they are worked through at an unconscious level.

The moral of this story is that a man has a rendezvous with death. But a man's obligation is to learn how to deal with the inevitable: with grace, grandeur and joy, with feast and sharing, not with fear and trembling. The worst thing that could happen to the Hispanic is to face death alone, without rituals, because that is the only way we can handle death—with dignity and grace.

All you have to do is to go to a hospital and see the Hispanic person. There are hundreds of people, relatives from everywhere—second cousins, third cousins, grandparents. Although their visits are only at a certain time, and for fifteen minutes, they bring food and flowers and animals and cheeses. Meanwhile, the sick person is moaning and groaning, but looking around to see who is there and taking names. When the people leave, he says, "How come so-and-so didn't come?" It is an obligation to pay tribute to death and to the dying because someday you will be dying yourself and will need this kind of support, like the bullfighter needs the audience to face the bull. He will not face the bull without that audience. He cannot perform.

Feelings of Ambivalence

We, as people in the Southwest, until recently were fairly content in continuing our way of life, dwelling on our religion, our poetry, our literature, our rather simple traditional ways, our family structure that prepared us for the inevitable. It was very clear to us that life was just a period in time. Now we are getting a taste of building a paradise on earth, of having a share of the earth's wealth, and that maybe heaven is not up there, but it might be here. We want to live to be 85 years old, like the rest of the people. We also want to be computer scientists, have Jaguars and Mercedes, and have good homes and travel. We want to learn different languages and to intermarry. This change is happening at an alarming rate and the impact of the epic myth is so overwhelming, especially now that we have an interesting media to sell it. All this is tearing us apart.

It is a very difficult struggle as we are trying to grab the thread of continuity. Like all struggles where there's such a radical transition at such an alarming pace, particularly this continuous kind of change, it leaves in the person a feeling of ambivalence about where we are heading. On the one hand, there is the destruction of our race, the end. We see this in our youth. On the other hand there is the good feeling of being able to share the rewards as San Antonio's mayor, Henry Cisneros, so beautifully demonstrates by the way he dresses, talks, and carries himself. Finally, a share in the epic! He is our best representative of the Epic Man: growth, movement, speculation, and industry. We also have a generation that is not so sure. When you get Henry Cisneros in the privacy of where we hang out, we see the other side of that man that he does not present to the public. He also is wondering what we will lose, what will disappear, what will be thrown into the mainstream. That ambivalence is there. How are we handling that?

Mythology as an Historical Solution

Historically, we were faced with similar problems. One problem surrounds the myth of the *Virgen de Guadalupe*, a powerful myth in our culture that is having a renaissance. The myth is currently significant because we are going back to religious institutions rapidly as one way of preserving our culture. What about this symbol? What is the role she has played in the history of Mexico that gives her the enormous power to galvanize and bring together people in a common cause?

The story begins about 450 years ago, when the first archbishop of Mexico, Bishop Umalga, a humble Franciscan and a defender of the Indian, struggled against the corrupt government of Spain and its atrocities toward the Indian. The Indians were on the verge of virtual annihilation because they were refusing to convert and they would rather choose death than give up their old gods. They were on the brink of annihilation, just as had happened in Peru and in other Latin American countries. There was a very humble Indian, Juan Diego, so the story goes, who was going to mass, and on his way to church he passed the little mound of Tepeyac. Juan Diego saw an image of what appeared to be an Indian goddess, but it was one that he was not familiar with; yet he recognized her as an Indian goddess. There was an image of this virgin standing in front of the rays of the sun being lifted by an angel standing on the crest of the moon. She was dressed in a garment of turquoise, a mantle that had stars all over it. Her hands were folded up and she was leaning toward the right. She was dark! Her eyes were looking down rather than straight like God's and she had a rope tied around her waist.

A recognized scholar, theologian Virgil Elizondo, pastor of San Fernando Cathedral in San Antonio, tells us that the Indians understood what all this meant. She was recognized as one of their own—dark-skinned. She was a goddess, but not like the other gods and goddesses in that she did not look straight out; she looked down as in compassion. The Indians believed that the eyes and the face were the windows to the soul, and this woman was in pain with a very caring and worried look, a compassionate look. Her mantle was turquoise, which is the color reserved for the principal god of the Indian people. And that god is androgenous which is both male and female and is the source of all life. The Indian was confused. Is this God, the real God, a loving God, a compassionate God?

The turquoise mantle was filled with stars. Stars indicated comets and comets announced new civilizations, new eras. This is how in the Indian mythology they would see that a new era would come to pass. As you look at the Aztec calendar, you see the eras that the Indian civilizations have gone through are based on the appearance and the disappearance of comets. They already knew that their civilization would end, but now this woman was announcing that there would be another era.

The position of the hands was not a position of prayer, but rather a greeting and an announcement—a great announcement! This is how the Indians announced a birth, or announced a new happening that had great consequences. The Indian saw that this woman was standing in front of the sun and the sun was one of their most important gods. She did not obliterate the sun, but she was obviously greater than the sun, and a continuation of the sun god. She was standing on top of the moon, so there was a connection with the god of night, but she was greater than the god of night because she was standing on top of the god of night and the god was sustaining her. There was a rope around her waist, the Indian sign of pregnancy.

So the meaning of the story is that your civilization will end, you people will end, but there will be a new civilization, a new people. I will give birth to a new race, and I will protect the one that's greater than the sun god, greater than the moon god, greater than your main god, and that brings love and compassion and peace.

Mythology of the Mexican American

Now, the rallying cry of today's leaders, particularly religious leaders, is a promise from the gods that we will survive as a people. There is a divine promise that a new race of people will be born. The

Mexican American now feels that this new race of people will come from the marriage of the epic people, the non-Hispanic and the Anglo American people, and us; marrying, mixing bloods, and out of this will come a new race of people—the Mexican American. If you look at that word it is very interesting. When I was a child if you looked at the little literature that was available, the word was always hyphenated. Now the hyphenation has been dropped. We see the symbolic merger of these two cultures, the ideas, the ways of life. The people from the epic cultures of mainstream American and the tragic cultures of the traditional Mexican American experience merge and there is the birth of a new race.

We are talking about the Southwest as the new paradise. Seeing the Southwest as the new nation of Aztlan. Aztlan is the ancient word for the Indian races, of our roots—the Southwest. The current American movement to the Southwest reinforces this belief.

This experience, this drama, this saga of the soul is very difficult to pinpoint and force into our methodologies of sociology, ethnohistory, and psychology, and I am having a difficult time trying to use the notion of paradise in my profession and to understand the inner soul of the Mexican American. However, this approach coincides with new thinking in these fields and anthropology. For example, Robert Lifton, Professor of Psychiatry at Yale, became famous for his writings on the Hiroshima and Nagasaki experience. He is toying around with dynamically-oriented psychiatry and psychology, the work of Freud and Adler, Jung, and Erikson, and bringing the work of mythology and anthropology together in a concept that is called symbolic formation. His theory is that the human mind needs to invent images, symbols, and myths in order to develop a sense of self and a sense of continuity. Once again scientists, sociologists and psychologists are looking at the process of myth-making, and a grand experience in the Southwest is being seen as the Mexican American struggles to move into the 20th century.

The role of myth making is profound. Just as profound is the discovery of the Mexican American mythology along with the upwardly mobile culture clashes and communication gaps experienced by these people. The role of Mexican American mythology and of the ultimate impact even on Third World countries promises to be an issue for future concern.

* *Edited from a taped transcription*

Ethnotherapy:
Healing the Wounds of
Ethnic Identity*
Price Cobbs, M.D.

I invite you to explore some of the concepts of ethnotherapy, particularly the causes of ethnic wounds. As a therapist, trying to heal the core of identity, it is clear to me that we have to delve deeper into ethnic issues. Some of the history involves the influence of my own background on the development of the concept of "ethnotherapy."

Background to the Development
of Ethnotherapy

I am a second generation physician from Los Angeles. My father was a physician during the depression and was very involved in social activism. In those days, he would have been described in the Los Angeles context as a "race man", somebody who at that time thought actively about race. He had a consciousness that was shaped out of being Black. It did not make him any more right or wrong than anyone else, but it was a perception. Much of my early life was spent in trying to figure out who I was and where I fit in. If you were Black, and did not have the usual economic credentials of being Black, that is, not on welfare and owning a car when you were in school, how did you put that into a racial context? And then, growing into adulthood during the civil rights movement and being exposed to the intellectual, the emotional, and very importantly, the moral giants of the late 1950's and early 1960's also affected me. My interest in multiculturalism clearly springs out of trying to understand something about being an "other" in this society. Always being different, and trying to understand what that meant.

In some of my early work in California I began to try to meld some of the issues of civil rights with what at that time was called the human potential movement. We discussed racial confrontation as a transcendental experience. It was fascinating. It was exciting. It was energizing. It more than exceeded our expectations. My late wife was working with me at that time. My kids, who are now in their thirties, remember it very vividly because they would wander around and come into rooms and see their father and mother yelling at white people, and white people yelling at their mother and father.

It was, I think, a real beginning in trying to put together a professional view after having been tremendously impacted and influenced by people like Dr. King, Malcolm X, and Cesar Chavez. It was a time when people were searching for their identity without being able to put their finger on it, except perhaps through some of the things that Erik Erikson was writing about; a time of trying to understand one's identity against a context of a broader world where the identities are different. Much of our scientific literature has focused on identity development without the impact of societies, religions, race, and gender. I think much of ethnotherapy is at least beginning to open that up, beginning to legitimize a more holistic view of ourselves.

The next real break through was my experience at the University of California, San Francisco, in the 1960's and early 1970's. There was an anti-war movement; there was a Black caucus; there was an Hispanic caucus; and our basic charge was to try to have a program of racial awareness and to focus on how we could reduce racism on campus. From that I began to look at how our basic assumptions about the races were distorted. This was apparent once we got into a room and began to talk with each other.

We also began to see a broader level of paranoia. As my own intellectual circle of practitioners began to get more international, I began to see that some of the paranoia that I thought was exclusively racial really had more to do with the psychology of the oppressed, with how people were acculturated in a society, with what they thought about themselves, and with what they thought about their own group. Finally, we became much more knowledgeable about projection, scapegoating, and the very essence of prejudice—bigotry, racism and sexism. We began to consider the therapeutic implications of ethnic exploration, so that we now define ethnotherapy as an addition to the therapeutic process that takes race, ethnicity, gender, and religion into account. It was not, however, without controversy.

In so much of my own training in San Francisco, I can remember going to case conferences as a young psychiatrist, where

I would be sitting with a group of social workers and psychologists. It would be as simple as someone who would start, "We have a case of a 45-year old woman." I would ask, "Black, Jewish, Irish Catholic or Italian?" As we continued I realized that my questions were being considered political rather than therapeutic.

I was always startled as I asked those questions because the response was invariably, "Oh, there he goes again. Well, I guess if you're Black and you're in this town, you have to ask those kinds of questions, and do your thing." I was really very aware that what I thought was central to my understanding of other human beings was not necessarily considered that essential, or might even be considered anti-therapeutic by others.

I was making a political statement. I think one of the things that gets dropped out as we talk about multiculturalism research and education is that by definition we are making a strong political statement in a world that needs reminding of the Holocaust, of Apartheid in South Africa, and of oppression around the world. When we talk about multiculturalism we are probing the melting pot concept and concentrating on how to understand differences. To many, this is controversial, therefore political.

The Ethnotherapeutic Process

How would we start such a process? As I look at the ethnotherapy process, I think of three levels: the individual, relationships, and the society.

The Personal Level

The first level, and to me a major aspect of multiculturalism, is to understand the personal. What were my first recollections of difference? That is a very individual question. For instance, I can almost categorically say that in this country if you grew up Black your first recollections of difference would be black/white. I remember vividly as I grew up my mother would drop her voice and say something about "the other group." She and my father might be in a very animated conversation about church or about this or that, and then I would hear my mother say "and the other group."

What is this? As I grew older I realized that that was our way, our family way, our cultural way of beginning to define who we were and who other people were. I want to underline that as she talked about "the other group," it was not with hostility. It certainly may have been with ambivalence and there may well have been feelings of rejection. It was really just a description—them and us. In therapy, I would want you to think about your first recollections of difference, and how they occurred.

Many times our first recollection of differences would be around religion, particularly for people in this country who may have grown up in the Northeast. So many of the Northeastern experiences, rather than racial, would be "we were Polish and they were Irish," or "I was very aware that we lived on this side of town where there were a group of Jewish kids and on the other side of town there was that parochial school that was Catholic." I think for many white people who grew up in the South, certainly their first recollection of difference would be Blacks vs.Whites.

So many times our first recollection of difference and the emotional charge connected with it are things that follow us the rest of our lives because we rarely go back and examine it. Rarely is difference thought of as emotionally neutral or even benign. Most of the time as we have grown up the metaphor for difference is invariably better or worse, particularly in a Western context. In a Western context invariably we compare and contrast, and we must develop the psychology and the semantics to begin to think of difference as simply *difference*.

So much of difference in this country is "bad guts," negative feelings that are difficult to understand. For instance, an ad for Schick razor blades had this punch line: "Sometimes to be different is to be better." It was fascinating because I was saying to myself, in order for that ad to be understood in a few seconds, it obviously had to be speaking right into a cultural consensus. The cultural norm would have to be "to be different is not to be better."

I think that many times as we get back into our personal time track, we can begin to get in touch with the feelings of religious bigotry, or racism, or sexism that we all have. This process can at least begin to give us some basis for how we began to form them. Where did I, in fact, get my feelings about work? Where did I get my work ethic? Where, in fact, did I get my value system? All of this is a very personal exploration, because so much of understanding multiculturalism is to begin to recognize that our values may have been formed differently. Clearly we may share many values, but it is where the values may be slightly different, or our timing may be slightly different, that we have the most difficulty. I would say that for me, the first process of ethnotherapy is this type of personal internal exploration.

The Interpersonal Level

The second part of the ethnotherapeutic process is the interpersonal. What goes on between me and other people? Think of yourself interacting with other people who are mostly similar to you. "I am 28, I am a woman, I grew up in England, my background is Angle Saxon." Also, think of yourself as dealing with someone just about like that, maybe a brother or sister. From there, begin to make it more and more different and see if you put your finger on what Malcolm X used to call the multiple roles we play as we move cross culturally. I see this in my own work as a consultant, with people who run large industries and who are paid enormous sums of money to effectively and efficiently run them. I might be with that person for one, two, three days, so I clearly get an opportunity to share intellectually, emotionally, and to really develop a healthy respect for someone's intellectual capacity. Then, I watch that same person as race or gender is introduced and the intellect falls off the tape. I think we equate sheer "smarts" with the ability to think multiculturally, and it does not work that way.

At the interpersonal level you constantly have to put your finger on "Where am I?" Am I intellectually blocked when I am dealing with someone whose skin color is different? Do I feel in my gut a churning when I know that the players have changed? I call it "the eggshell syndrome," and all of us feel it. As a Black person, I feel it many times as I interact with other people. People get literally robbed of spontaneity because of the eggshells. I say this as a mature person who has empathy for my own and other peoples' eggshells.

We may feel multiculturally sophisticated with sexism or civil rights and then we realize that we have just scratched the surface, that we really are in fact talking about something that is lifelong. In my work there is a feeling that no anti-semitism exists. For example, "Okay, now that we are so aware about minorities and a multicultural work force, it is okay for me to tell you that joke about a Jewish guy I met last week." So much of that thinking contributes to and perpetuates the eggshells at the interpersonal interface. I would ask you, as you slow it down, to begin thinking. How in fact do I feel emotionally as I deal with difference? How have I incorporated those different people with whom I have come in contact, with whom I have lived over the years?

The Social Level

Finally, at the third level of ethnotherapy, I would invite you to look at the environment, our society. What is the effect of multiculturalism? How do we do things with it? Another chapter in this book discusses a multicultural city—San Antonio. How does it differ from Minneapolis? How does it differ culturally from Fargo, North Dakota? How does it differ from places that might have 50,000 people or in the Midwest where the ethnic base has either been assimilated, or has been denied or has not been able to be expressed? Do I see myself reflected in my environment as it relates to me? So much of ethnocentrism is the feeling that what happens to me in a culture happens to everyone else. That is really not true.

I will never forget an experience I had at the end of my first year at medical school in 1955, going to the Jefferson Hotel in St. Louis. That was at a time when integration was just beginning and was very tentative. One did not know where to go. We had driven from Nashville to St. Louis and looked like students. So we had on whatever students were wearing during those days. We walked into the Jefferson Hotel and you could have heard a pin drop as we walked up to the counter. "Sorry, sir, we're having an insurance convention here, love to have you but we're crowded." We threatened with the NAACP (National Association for the Advancement of Colored People) and all those things that we could threaten with, and then we got in our car and went to the local Black motel and spent the night. Several months later I was in St. Louis again, although this time I had come by plane and I had on a suit and tie. I went to the same hotel; at that point I could project a certain kind of professionalism that at least fit into the class system in some way. And, oh, the red carpet! I would have thought it was one of the better hotels in St. Louis. "Fine sir, we're glad to have you." You were glad to be in, but you knew you were being patronized. The social context had changed and behaviors changed accordingly.

Wounds That Need Ethnic Healing

The consequences of such experiences result in ethnic wounds. I will mention only six briefly.

Psychology of the Oppressed

First, there really is a psychology of the oppressed. People who grow up feeling oppressed, particularly feeling oppressed as a member of a category, invariably develop a comparable psychology. There is a psychology that accrues as one grows up, as part of that group that is trying to get in. One is invariably matched against a mythical value. For black people, the value is to get an education. *"They* cannot take it away from you." "You are going to have to work twice as hard to get the same results." I am certain all of you will begin to think of your own internal messages; internal with you, internal in terms of family.

I remember having conversations with people about table manners. All of us, certainly if we have kids, review all of our own training around table manners, and we are either going to make our kids better or worse. I remember thinking it was such a uniquely Black experience. However, after talking with people who were not Black, I realized they have the same problem. "You've got to be prepared when you do so and so because *they* will be looking at you." When you realize that it is the whole subsurface of people trying to "get in" who obviously want to share common experiences, but do so by comparing themselves with some intangible group that they can never quite identify. What does this do? How does it affect you?

Feeling Devalued

The first thing that happens, and this is a wound that we have to look at, is that it fosters ambivalence and self-doubt. Self-doubt about oneself and about the society occurs, and self-doubt clearly conveys and promotes devaluation. So much of understanding the psychology of the oppressed is to understand devaluation. People like me feel devalued; therefore, all of us are devalued.

Aggression and the Survival Mindset

To begin understanding something around ethnic wounds is to see aggressiveness in a reactive rather than a proactive way. So much of the aggressiveness that we see in people who have been oppressed is that many times it is used to lash out, to get back, to survive, but rarely to master. Much of ethnotherapy is helping people get in touch with their ability to master. The need is often very crucial, and quite subtle. The solution, though difficult, is to help people begin to incorporate and take survival as a gift. How do

I help this person who is really having problems surviving economically, emotionally, socially and psychologically to incorporate a feeling that survival is a given?

There are so few people who are oppressed who take survival as a gift that they were one step off from welfare. A critical point in the therapeutic process for the therapist is to realize that this individual, for all his training and experience, psychologically feels one step off of welfare. That connotes a survival mindset. A mindset of mastery says, "I am going to be on welfare, and if I am, I'll change its name." That is, a mastery orientation sees being on welfare as a temporary situation that will soon be overcome.

Lack of Historical Continuity

Another wound that we have to understand is a lack of a sense of historical continuity. We, as Americans, are ahistoric. Not having historical continuity is so graphic a cultural phenomenon that the fallout is just beginning to be appreciated. This lack of historical continuity has profound consequences particularly for ethnic minorities. Those of us who consider ourselves oppressed discover that a lack of a sense of historical accomplishment both on the individual level and on the group level results in a lack of historical identity. This is another wound that we have to understand more fully: The impact of historical discontinuity on ethnic identity.

Rage

Rage to me is the downside of any oppression. I remember years ago being on a committee of the Joint Commission for the Mental Health of Children. It was in the late 1960's and it was a diverse group—Native Americans, Chicanos, Puerto Ricans, northern and southern Whites, and a couple of Asians. When I was talking about rage, I had an intellectual mindset that somehow rage was related only to the historical circumstances of Blacks, and that rage did not occur within other groups. However, it became clear to me that rage is, in fact, on a continuum, and part of that continuum is rage turned inward. Examples multiply including the Native American reservations or the barrios in San Antonio where we could go to see rage turned inward. To understand ethnicity is to understand something about healing the wounds of anger turned inward into rage.

Lack of Empowerment

Finally, another aspect of understanding ethnotherapy has to do with wounds coming from low feelings of empowerment. This issue may be crucial within the next decade. Robert Coles, the Harvard psychiatrist, staked his claim on looking at the oppressed. He has studied children in school integration situations; Chicano children in the Southwest; Alaskan and Aleutian children; he studied poor white children in Kentucky, and finally, he studied affluent children. It was fascinating that among the affluent kids he really began to look at that old psychological notion of entitlement. Affluence does something to its children, leaving them with a mindset that the affluent have more rights to things than the average person, rights that other children do not have.

We have only touched the hem of the ethnotherapy garment. But my belief is that by understanding the levels of ethnotherapy and the psychological wounds of the oppressed we are in a better professional posture to train, educate, research—and to heal.

* Edited from a taped transcription

Developing Intercultural Self-Worth
Patrick Flores, Archbishop of San Antonio

It is important to learn techniques of how to accept yourself and then to be able to accept others who are different from you. What makes a person beautiful is that there are no two people alike. Some are skinny, some are fat, some are tall, some are short and some are different colors. It is this diversity that makes people great.

In my travels of over two-thirds of the world in my 55 plus years, the one thing that impresses me is that no other person looks like me. I do not need to get tired of myself because every time I see someone else, I see someone different. When I say that I have found everybody else different, I am not saying that they are any worse than I am, nor any better. Being different does not mean that the other human being comes from a worse class or a better class. He or she is just different. The beauty of all this is the fact that we have been made by nature, by our fathers and mothers and, we say, by the Almighty God. Each one of us is uniquely beautiful and uniquely great, so there's no reason we need to apologize. We're okay. As we discover that we are okay, we discover that others who happen to be different are okay, too.

Self-Worth Through Understanding Differences

I will share some experiences that have confirmed my conviction that there is great value in us being who we are and learning to accept and to work with others who are different. Recently, there was an article in one of the local papers criticizing a practice that has been taking place in a little town on the American side of the border between the United States and Mexico. The writer had visited on All Soul's Day and had taken pictures of people going to the cemetery, taking a plate of food—the best that they had—and then putting it on the grave of the mother, the father, the brother, the sister; any dear one that had died. The article was actually negative, saying that this is horrible, pagan and old fashioned. It even said those people have had a priest teaching them for over a hundred years and they have not yet broken their pagan ways. I read the article, but I did not give it much attention.

Three days later a lady came into my office; she was so upset that she did not even wait her turn. She rushed in, wanting to get this whole thing straightened out. She began by saying, "I cannot stand to have this taking place in Texas; it's a horrible thing for a group of Mexican people who are Catholic in the valley of Texas to be taking a plate of food to their dead." She continued, "Do they still believe that the dead can eat, don't they believe that the dead are dead and that's it? If the bishop there has not done anything about it, you, as Archbishop, should put a stop to it immediately." And so, she really let me have it in no uncertain terms.

She continued to talk, which gave me time to do some thinking. Then when she finally came to a break, I said, "Lady, has anyone died in your family?"

She said, "Oh, yes, my mother died about a year ago."

"Well, when she died, didn't you take some beautiful flowers to the funeral home and maybe you placed a spray of flowers on her casket? And when you buried her, didn't you put any flowers in the cemetery?"

She said, "Oh yes, I did, but you know, my mother's favorite flowers were the black orchids, they're very scarce." She said, "They're very expensive, so for her funeral we had a big spray of black orchids. It was very expensive."

Then I said, "Why? Did she smell them, did she eat them, did she see them, wasn't she dead already?" I was going to go on, but when I said "why?" I simply waited.

Then, before I said much more she said, "Oh, I understand what you mean."

I said, "But I still want to say what I mean. What's worse, taking a plate of food and placing it on the grave of a dear one, or taking flowers? Which do the dead enjoy most? I believe that we don't stop loving our dear ones when they die, and we search for ways to express our love. Now here, most of us express our way with flowers, but some people express their way with food. Isn't it true, that when you really love somebody who's alive you invite them to come and join you at table? Sharing your table, isn't that a way of sharing your love?"

What everyone is trying to say is that we love our deceased relatives and friends, but we have different ways of expressing our love. When she left she said, "I really came here to tear you apart, but I am happy that you have put me together." I simply asked her to share with others the fact that we are not the only ones who do things the right way.

Recently, I had another visitor from one of the countries in Africa. He was telling me that he never gives a flower to another person. He said, "We have wild flowers all over, but we never give a flower to another person because we wouldn't give them something they cannot eat. Now, we give food; we give candy; we give this and the other. That's why we also place food on the graves of our dead; that is our way of giving them something that we wish they could eat. That's the way we would express our love."

Very often the mistake that we make is to conclude that we do things right, but anyone who does things differently is wrong, or perhaps old fashioned. Actually, if we share with one another why we do do things in different ways, we will find out that each way is okay. Other ways can enrich our way if we are willing to accept input.

Finding a Cultural Identity

There is a growth that I think is taking place in young people. On a high school retreat five years ago, I wanted to do an exercise with the students. I asked them to take 20 minutes of silence, a piece of paper and a pencil and walk around the grounds of the facility we were using, thinking of a person that they admire, that they wished they could be like.

The very first name that appeared, probably because his birthday had just been celebrated, was Elvis Presley. Half of the girls wanted to be like Elvis Presley. The second name they mentioned was President Kennedy. Most of the high schoolers were not born when Kennedy was assassinated, but they had read about him, their parents had told them about him, and some of them wanted to be like him. There were two or three that wanted to be like me, but not as fat, they said.

After about seven minutes, the blackboard was filled with names of people they all wanted to be like. When everyone had expressed or shared the name of the person he or she admired, I took chalk and made a big X over the names. And I said, "In case you don't know it, I must tell you that you can never accomplish that. You can never become like another human being, no matter what you do to yourself. My biggest disappointment is that not one of you said, 'I want to be myself.' Why in the process of thinking of big and wonderful people didn't you think of yourself? Aren't you big enough, aren't you wonderful enough, aren't you great enough?" Then, as they began to share, they explained the fact they had a very poor self-image.

That exercise was significant because shortly before, I had been called in the middle of the night to three homes where the families had returned home and found one of their children had committed suicide. All three of them had left notes that were almost identical: "I don't want to go on living because I know I ain't good." They were saying, "We do not want to live because we know we are no good, unworthy and undeserving of being loved and of loving."

We need to take a very deep look at ourselves and discover the greatness that is in us, who we really are, and not have to apologize to anybody for being who we are. Blacks do not have to apologize for being black, whites do not have to apologize for being white, browns do not have to apologize for being brown, orientals do not have to apologize for having eyes the way they have them. What is wrong with us the way we are?

Not too long ago, I went to Germany in the middle of the winter. The area that I was in was covered with snow, but one day the sun came out and I couldn't believe what I saw that morning. The German people were in bikinis and bathing suits with towels, laying on the snow. They would lie on the towels for 20 minutes or so to get a suntan. But the weather was nineteen degrees below zero and I was wearing the biggest overcoat that I owned trying to keep warm! And then they saw me. They immediately came to ask me where I got my suntan. I simply said that God gave it to me; what's wrong with it? They were white wanting to become black or brown. At other times I've seen blacks using Ajax trying to become white. And I've told a lot of women "I love you the way you are, you don't have to paint yourself up." There are also men my age trying to buy wigs and hair pieces. What is wrong with being baldheaded?

Let us really look at ourselves and discover that there's nothing in me and nothing in you for which we have to apologize. We are okay; we are great; we are wonderful. We're living images of the living God. My insistence on that is for this purpose: I am expected to accept all others and to accept the greatness in other people. However, I cannot accept the greatness in other people if I do not accept the fact that I am okay. It has to begin with me. Now, the moment that I am convinced that I am okay, then I do not have any problem saying that all of you are equally great. If I were to have a very low self-image of myself and if I were to continue with that, then I would want to get rid of every one of you. If I discover my value, my goodness and my greatness, then I can see the goodness and the greatness in all of you.

I think that there has been a change in the self-image of teenagers. Five years ago kids wanted to be everybody else. I did the same experiment several times in the last two or three months, and I was pleasantly surprised. When I asked them to write the name of a great person in their life, most of the teenagers wrote their mothers, fathers, or themselves. When I asked, "But why do you see your mothers and fathers as being great and wonderful?"

They said, "Because I'm great; they must be great too, because I'm part of them." I thought their reasoning was beautiful. At that point, I was able to perceive other things: the animosity, the fighting, the jealousy, and the envy that was there five years ago had melted. The young people were willing to hold hands. They were willing to hold hands regardless of whether they were black or white, Vietnamese, Cambodian, Korean, Polish American, Czech American, German American, Filipino American, or whatever. They were holding hands as equals.

The rapid speed of transportation and communication puts us at each other's back yards instantly. Therefore, I think it is particularly important in this age for us to grow in our awareness of the diversity in the family of nations. We must be aware of the value of this diversity, and that we become richer when we share with others.

We must not lose who we are. We must want to continue to be ourselves while allowing others to share themselves with us. Every group of people has some greatness that can enrich the lives of others, if it is shared. Intercultural sharing among peoples is a goal towards which we all should strive!

Cross-Cultural Reentry

Clyde N. Austin, Ph.D.

Johan Bojer, in *The Emigrants* (1925), poignantly stated:

If you came back, you wanted to leave again; if you went away, you longed to come back. Wherever you were, you could hear the call of the homeland, like the note of a herdsman's horn far away in the hills. You had one home out there, and one over here, and yet you were an alien in both places. Your true abiding-place was the vision of something very far off, and your soul was like the waves, always restless, forever in motion (p.351).

As one reflects upon moving to a culture foreign to one's existence and upon the return, the incisive question arises, "Where *is* my home?" The reentry process is never easy, but it can be a time of productive growth. Werkman (1980) observed, "The task of readapting to the United States after living overseas is, for many, the most difficult hurdle in the cycle of international life" (p. 233).

The Challenge

The challenge before us as researchers, trainers, and managers is to keep the expatriates (family members *and* singles) psychologically spiritually, socially, and financially whole throughout the foreign cycle. Our view *must* encompass the expatriate *and* each member of his or her family in view of institutional policy *and* individual career paths. Scrutinizing attention must be given to each dimension of recruitment, selection, training, on-the-field support, and reentry. In essence, I am calling for an allencompassing view of the total intercultural cycle. As Adler (1981) aptly said, "Sending failures will not bring home successes" (p. 354).

Two studies which reflect our challenge are those of Foyle (1984) and Young (1980). Dr. Marjory Foyle, speaking at the Seminar on Mental Health of Missionaries, London, England

(1984), summarized data collected from visits made to Bangladesh, Pakistan and Nepal between January, 1982, and April, 1983. From the records of 80 patients seen in detail, she reported a division of patients into four groups:

1. Those with *no psychiatric symptomology* . They required simple counseling for a straightforward problem—13/80, (16%).

2. Those with *age-related psychiatric symptoms* , i.e., those who would have developed these symptoms wherever they were working—2/80, (3%)

3. Those with *psychiatric symptoms present before selection* —28/80, (35%).

4. Those with *stress-related psychiatric symptoms*—37/80, (46%).

Young conducted a comprehensive evaluation of Canada World Youth (CWY) participants. (CWY participants spent five months in training and five months in their cross-cultural assignments.) "A slight majority of respondents reported initial difficulty in coming home" (p. 8). At the time of the study, about 40 percent of the respondents felt that they were still having readjustment problems.

Lest we be afflicted with psychological "tunnel vision," there is another facet to our challenge—the application of what we learn about reentry to problems within our own country. Dr. Brent Ruben suggested to me in a telephone conversation that we probably need to think in terms of a generic stress phenomenon which occurs in a spectrum of transitional experiences. One article which exemplifies this range of experiences is D. P. Jansson's (1975). She wrote about the common social process shared by individuals such as ex-convicts, former mental patients, and ex-clergy in their return to society. Too, our research in this area might lead to helpful insights for mothers reentering the world of work. In the summer of 1979 Hahnemann Medical School in Philadelphia was developing an exemplary reentry counseling program for prison inmates and their spouses. I had the privilege of attending one of these counseling sessions and talking with the program director. About six months prior to the actual release date, weekly sessions were conducted by a therapist with the couple in an appropriate therapeutic setting.

Jansson stated that the reentrant is in a minority. Because of society's lack of information about such processes, the reentrant may acquire, through no fault of *his/her* own, a "deviant identity." According to Opubor (1974), "In both the host and home cultures, the individual will be something of a deviant. The most edifying choice for the individual, and the goal of all constructive strategy, is how to make the individual a responsible deviant" (p. 29). Even a college professor who takes a sabbatical might be considered "a responsible deviant."

Psychological Problems Upon Reentry

For a significant number of repatriates, psychological difficulties emerge from a web of commonly recognized problem areas such as academic, cultural, social, political, linguistic, and professional. I have chosen *not* to address each of these potentially difficult areas. Rather, I would like to provoke you to thoughtfully contemplate the *psychological* costs of repatriation. As a result of my professional practice, my research, my work as a professional psychologist in Buenos Aires, Argentina, my service experience during the Korean War and eight years of teaching experience at Dyess Air Force Base, Texas, I am convinced that many families have been shamed to silence by negative attitudes toward mental illness evidenced by relatives, friends, and colleagues. In many situations, there has been a conspiracy of silence!

We need to "let the singles and families speak." They need to know that they are not alone—that many other returnees have similar problems. Then their sponsor and society need to provide the reorientation and/or counseling which will permit them to become whole again. Returnees have developed valuable skills which would immeasurably enrich the people and operations of their sponsors.

In my judgment, too many problems are ignored or "swept under the rug." They are hidden from corporate or agency eyes! Recently, when visiting with a major governmental official in Country X, the male official said, "We don't have any significant reentry problems." Immediately after my wife, Sheila, and I left his office, we talked with a woman in the same bureau who volunteered opposing views!

In the summer of 1984, we visited with a corporate family in a major European city. The wife told us about bridge parties for North

American corporate wives where valium was passed around like M & M's!

Some officials are uninformed, and their agencies are poorly funded. Last year, Sheila and I visited with the top personnel official of a large missions agency. After I described our research and some of the practical measures we are advocating, I asked for his observations. I could sense that he was groping for an adequate response. Eventually he said, "You have given me a sense of profound guilt about our lack of provision for our missionaries." Obviously, it was *not* our intent to make him feel guilty. He was soberly reflecting on his responsibility to his personnel.

Brown and Streator (1974) estimated that the Department of State, AID, and USIA foreign affairs employees had 11,000 children at, or below, college age. Of that number, they felt that approximately 1,900 children in the Foreign Service community had potential needs in 1974. Shiner (1974) reported that 8,000 American Defense Department children return to the USA each year. According to her, about 10 percent of these TCK's (Third Culture Kids) possess readjustment problems serious enough to require counseling.

In an attempt to secure more up-to-date data, I contacted the Family Liaison Office and Medical Division, Employee Consultation Services, Department of State. When I inquired about current statistics on the reentry problems of children, I was told that there were no recent studies. However, one official said, "Informally, we know the need is there." Another official stated, "In my judgment the problem is greater than in 1974."

Unfortunately, reentry is too often considered only in job-related, financial and logistical terms—"nuts and bolts." I have read many articles discussing questions such as: How much will it cost to comfortably relocate a family to a stateside home? Should we provide up-to-date information on automobiles? Should a relocation pay supplement be provided? Will we give annual leave *in advance* upon return? How much will it cost to relocate the family's pets and wine cellar? Most of these considerations are important but not to the exclusion of human costs. My unspoken response has been, "But what about the people?"

What *are* the human costs? How can we measure the traumatic impact on a family network when a repatriate child spends a year in a mental hospital? Can a family easily recover from a teen-age abortion?

The Primacy of the Self-Concept

On the eve of reentry, the question "Who am I?" may perplex the repatriate. Meintel (1971) argued, "The most significant 'shocks' potential in strangerhood are those of self-discovery" (p. 47). Mason's provocative dissertation (1978) lucidly traced the development of China missionary sons and daughters. As these children attempted to move into the mainstream of USA life, self-discovery was a continuing process punctuated by expressions of social justice. In any major transition in life, to question self intensively is appropriate. Reentry is no exception. With a more accurate knowledge of one's self, comes a relaxed acceptance of self (Smalley, 1963, p. 56). To me, remolding of the reentrant's self-concept is the veritable bedrock issue of successful reentry.

Do families know how to cope with social retardation in their children or a period of delayed adolescence? According to Dr. Gordon Parsons ("Elite?", 1974), regional officer in the Department of State: "Our children are usually three to four years socially retarded." Dr. Ruth Useem (personal communication, November 9, 1981) has suggested that some returning children experience a delayed adolescence. Rather than moving through adolescence from the chronological ages of 13-18, Dr. Useem states that adolescence may extend from ages 20-28.

Dr. Useems's thinking seems to be supported by the research and practical clinical work of personality theorist Erik Erikson (1962) and the research of Dr. J. P. Wilson (1978) at Cleveland State University on reentering Vietnam veterans. Erikson set forth a series of eight stages in a psychological theory of development. Of primary importance for our consideration is the fifth psychosocial stage, Identity vs. Role Confusion, which occurs in late adolescence and young adulthood. The central developmental task of this stage is the formation of a more stable and enduring personality structure and a positive sense of self in order to constructively confront the tasks of adulthood. Erikson (1962) stated:

> Societies, knowing that young people can change rapidly, even in their most intense devotions, are apt to give them a *moratorium*, a span of time after they have ceased being children, but before their deeds and works count toward a

future identity. In Luther's time the monastery was, at least for some, one possible psychosocial moratorium, one possible way of postponing the decision as to what one is and is going to be. . . .The crisis in such a young man's life may be reached exactly when he half realizes that he is fatally overcommitted to what he is not (p. 43).

In cueing on Erikson, Wilson continued:

. . .the moratorium may take different forms in different cultures. . .If all goes well, then childhood identifications get transformed into a more or less crystallized sense of identity (p. 7).

In the Vietnam War, the average age of a USA soldier was between 19 and 20. For these men, the process of identity formation and the psychosocial moratorium was drastically disrupted. Wilson continued:

The results of our study suggest that *within* each succeeding psychosocial crisis, the veteran will be faced with the additional developmental task of rethinking, reconceptualizing or reforming his thoughts, images and emotions of Vietnam with regard to the following issues: a) his own identity, motivational orientation, value system and moral adjustment perspective; b) the quality, type and degree of interpersonal involvement; c) authority relations and the perceptions of institutions in society and the nature of the political process (p. 136).

In his superb dissertation, Downie (1976) noted that TCK's rarely view home and roots as being located in their country of citizenship. In working with TCK's, and, I suspect, Third Culture Adults, (TCA's), it is important to keep in mind that these Third Culture Persons (TCP's) maintain what Downie described as an "inner continuity inclusive of their third culture experience while maintaining a social identity intended to approximate one which is relevant to the new environment" (p. 234). TCK's are "a part of and apart from" the American high school and/or college social scene. Downie continued, "In search for identity, the life plan becomes vital. . . . Involvement in some aspect of the third culture becomes a central feature of their life planning" (p. 235).

Werkman (1978) reported that one of his young clients used the term "culture dsyphoria syndrome" to describe his feelings. He was anxious, depressed and restless. The client wrote:

Once you realize you can never penetrate the hermetically sealed, parochial xenophobia of the natives here in the United States, you breathe a sigh of despair mixed with relief and set out toward a native country you know you must create for yourself, inside (p. 126).

Another said: "I'm two people. The one who uses English is quiet and precise; the Portuguese one gestures and is poetic and free" (p. 125).

A Sense of Loss

Another prevailing motif of reentry is a sense of loss. Werkman (1978) suggested that deeply experienced loss might result in a kind of freezing of psychological maturation and a lack of openness to new experiences.

Moore (1981) discovered, in a study of 288 returned missionaries, that the second most difficult problem listed was "nostalgia and homesickness" for the mission field. Jansson (1975) graphically sketched what she calls a "sense of powerlessness" (p. 139). Useem (Personal Communication, November 9, 1981) affirmed, "The loss of an elite status is very difficult for parents." Zimmerman (1970) mourned, "What is most disturbing is a sense of loss. Where is the America I left four years ago? What has happened to Washington? The changes are so terrifying that it is hard to accept reality as real" (p.38). The sense of loss is heightened by the lack of interest displayed by sponsors. Frank (1975) revealed, in a study of 120 returning Missionary Aviation Fellowship personnel, that in *no* case did the reentrant receive *any* help in rehabilitation from his home church.

Werkman (1972) recounted the *dramatic* loss of Rudyard Kipling, suffered in reverse, as written by Edmund Wilson:

Kipling grew up in India with his parents and adoring native servants until he was six. His parents then decided to send him home to England for schooling and to live with his uncle, but did not explain to him the reason for their plan. Kipling became morose in England and spent endless hours staring out of the window of his uncle's house. He developed partial blindness and a "severe nervous breakdown" (p. 99).

The sense of loss is pictured in an expressive manner by several representative repatriates:

I am still not comfortable shopping here. It's not so much the variety, which some returned missionaries find daunting, but the lack of what I want. I can't stand canned things. I like to buy just fresh fruits and vegetables.

I wish we could walk more. It's no wonder everyone has trouble with their weight here. So many of the streets don't even have sidewalks. Why is this such a motorized society?

I'd forget to sweep the floor. It never occurred to me. I'd not cleaned house in the Middle East for eight years. It almost felt degrading to clean my home. I looked for a maid—couldn't find one.

I miss taking time for people.

In the summer of 1968, my father was involved in an automobile accident on his way home from a tent campaign in the northern hill country of Antonio. Unfortunately, the accident accelerated his kidney disease. We returned to the USA. Leaving that country was a traumatic experience, especially for a 13-year-old boy who was not fluent in English and was leaving everything he loved. By the age of 10, the only thing that distinguished me from a citizen of Antonio was my blue eyes and blond hair. Adjusting to the American scene was extremely difficult; it was as if I had completely missed seven years of my life.

Mrs. Isabel Burn (1978) of Foxton, England, has developed the only study I know of which highlights grief as the central thesis. She and her husband, Dr. R.P. Burn, a professor of Homerton College, Cambridge served as missionaries in India for 10 years. Mrs. Burn said, "Meeting and talking to other missionaries who had returned. . .showed me that I was not alone in feeling disoriented and bereaved" (p. 1). Onethird of those replying stated they had no difficulties in adjusting; the other 66 percent had difficulties of various kinds. Onethird of the total number had spiritual and emotional problems. "For most of this latter group, the difficulties bore the marks of a bereavement experience" (p. 20).

Value, Change and Choice

Clashes in inner values may occur between homecomers and "receivers" in bewildering arenas: material possessions, family life, racial prejudice, national priorities in areas of ecology and politics, and Christian community conflicts. Sensitivity must prevail on both sides of what might be a considerable chasm in values if a "common pool of hurt" (Morrow, 1981, p. 19) is to be avoided.

Interviews with returning missionaries, as well as formal studies (Bwatwa, Ringenberg, Wolde and Mishler, 1972; Moore, 1981) indicate that missionaries experience the USA as possessing "an embarrassment of riches." One missionary mother returning from the Far East said:

> Everybody looks rich to us. We stayed with good friends in a Western state who complained about the high cost of living. Yet, they are overweight; live like royalty. Many people talk about inflation and how they are cutting corners, . . .but most are wasteful and keep on buying. Why is air conditioning kept so low? We freeze everywhere we go.

Simcox (1976) said:

> I had forgotten the well-groomed, proper look of the American landscape. It is as if each blade of grass dares grow unplanned. . .In a way it is a humbling experience to return. . .it seems almost presumptuous to claim to represent it abroad. . . .It is the all-pervading affluence of the US that most impresses the returning diplomat. . .(p. 21).

> Can a nation become "overdeveloped," if that term has any validity? Is the average individual American now approaching the outer limits of his capacity to consume the flood of goods, services, and amusements the American cornucopia is capable of dropping on him?. . .What does such a uniquely rich nation have to say to the rest of the world? (p. 22).

Consider my own example. San Antonio occupies a special niche in our hearts. It was here that I purchased my wife's engagement ring. It was in San Antonio that I first taught school—North East High School. And it was here that we returned from Argentina. After being processed through Customs at the International Airport, we drove to Luby's Cafeteria in the nearby

North Star Mall for lunch. It was December, 1971. The Mall glistened with the materialism of our society. I was overwhelmed; I cried!

What Can We Do?

1. Acquaint oneself with the literature, perhaps by beginning with reading and re-reading Judith N. Martin's comprehensive article (1984) entitled "The Intercultural Reentry: Conceptualization and Directions for Future Research." In addition to the literature specifically on reentry, we need to competently review materials in areas such as transition, mobility, stress, and man's development cycle. I have searched more than twenty data bases in two countries. As a consequence of the research, I have made a lengthy list of research needs. I would like to share five of these at this time:

   a. To the best of my knowledge, there are only two longitudinal studies of expatriates.

   b. There are few studies of reentering *adults*, regardless of sponsorship.

   c. To the best of my knowledge, there are no studies which have *focused* on mental health problems of expatriate families.

   d. What are the pertinent in-the-field variables which make a successful reentry? (e.g., such as urban or rural setting; length of stay overseas; number of moves; language proficiency; type of overseas education; geographical location; socio-economic status; reentry of citizens of many countries—USA, Canada, England and Japan).

   e. How are the cross-cultural talents of returning adults used by their respective groups?

2. Within the corporate or governmental sectors, management needs to be sensitive to research needs on reentry. They could offer to fund such research. Valid longitudinal research studies on reentry are few in number. Dr. Maurice Lipsedge and Dr. Ricky Caplan, London, England, are currently conducting a significant longitudinal study.

3. Universities can establish relocation centers. Fontaine (1983) describes the thrust of the University of Pittsburgh in this respect.

4. More consulting firms should add reentry workshops to their repertoires.

5. Organizational representatives should encourage the publication of in-house studies. Have they tried to "rap the chain of command" for a study? In some cases, it is like attempting to nail Jello to the wall!

6. We need more training centers like the new $20 million Missionary Learning Center of the Foreign Mission Board of the Southern Baptist Convention.

7. We need a national clearinghouse or clearinghouses on selected research topics.

References

Adler, N. J. "Re-entry: Managing Cross-Cultural Transitions". *Group and Organization Studies.* v. 6, n. 3. pp. 341-356. 1981.

Bojer, J. *The Emigrants.* New York: Century Co. 1925.

Brown, M. J., and Streator, P. "An Advocate for the Kids." *Foreign Service Journal.* v. 51, n. 4. pp. 19-20; 26-27. 1974.

Burn, I. *Resettlement of Missionaries.* England. 1978. (Unpublished manuscript for a Certificate in Pastoral Theology, Cambridge University.)

Bwatwa, J., Ringenberg, R., Wold, N., and Mishler, J. "A Study of the Adjustment of Missions and Service Personnel Returning from Overseas Assignments." (Methods of Social Research, Sociology, 412). Goshen College, 1972. (Unpublished manuscript.)

Downie, R.D. *"Reentry Experiences and Identity Formation of Third Culture Experienced Dependent American Youth: An Exploratory Study"* . Dissertation Abstracts International, v. 37, n. 3493A. 1976. (University Microfilms Nr. 76-27,089.)

"Elite? Not Back to the USA". *To The Point.* Jan. 18. p. 35. 1974.

Erikson, E. *Young Man Luther: A Study in Psychoanalysis and History.* New York: Norton. 1962.

Fontaine, C. M. "International Relocation: A Comprehensive Psychosocial Approach". *EAP Digest*. March/April. pp. 27-31. 1983.

Foyle, M. F. *Seminar on Mental Health of Missionaries*. London. 1984. (Address to the Evangelical Missionary Alliance Conference on the Mental Health of Missionaries.)

Frank, T. *Resettlement Problems Faced by Missionaries Returning to the U.K. Before Retirement Age*. 1975. (Report to Birneck College, University of London.)

Jansson, D. P. "Return to Society: Problematic Features of the Re-Entry Process." *Perspectives in Psychiatric Care*. v. 13, n. 3. pp. 136-142. 1975.

Martin, J. N. "The Intercultural Reentry: Conceptualization and Directions for Future Research." *International Journal of Intercultural Relations*. n. 8. pp. 115-134. 1984.

Mason, S. M. R. *Missionary Conscience and the Comprehension of Imperialism: A Study of the Children of American Missionaries to China, 1900-1949*. Diss. Northern Illinois University. 1978. Dissertation Abstracts International. v. 39, n. 5105A-5106A. 1978. (University Microfilms n. 79-02,454.)

Meintel, D. "Strangers, Homecomers and Ordinary Men". *Anthropological Quarterly*. v. 46, n. 1. pp. 47-58. 1971.

Morrow, L. "The Forgotten Warriors". *Time*. July 13. pp. 18-25. 1981.

Moore, L. A. *A Study of Reverse Culture Shock in North American Church of Christ Missionaries*. Thesis. Abilene Christian University, 1981: *Masters Abstracts*. v. 20, n. 314. 1982. (University Microfilms. n. 13-18,268.)

Opubor, A. E. *Intercultural Adaptation: Resocialization Versus Reacculturation?* Racine, WI, 1974. (Paper presented to the Reentry/Transition Workshop at Wingspread).

Shiner, G. "Third Culture Kids Feel Like Foreigners in Their Own Country". *Richmond Times-Dispatch*. Dec. 8. p. F-3. 1974.

Simcox, D. E. "My Own, My Affluent Homeland". *Foreign Service Journal*. v. 44, n. 8. pp. 21-23; 46. 1967.

Smalley, W. A. "Culture Shock, Language Shock and the Shock of Self-Discovery". *Practical Anthropology*, 10. pp. 49-56. 1963.

Werkman, S. L. "Hazards of Rearing Children in Foreign Countries." *American Journal of Psychiatry*, 128. n. 8. pp. 106-11. 1972.

Werkman, S. L. "Coming Home: Adjustment of Americans to the United States After Living Abroad". *Uprooting and Development: Dilemmas of Coping with Modernization.* Eds. G. V. Coelho and P. I. Ahmed. New York: Plenum, 1980.

Wilson, J. P. *Identity, Ideology and Crisis: The Vietnam Veteran in Transition, Parts I and Parts II.* Cleveland State University, 1978. (Cincinnati, OH: Disabled American Veterans).

Young, W. *Youth and Development: A Follow-up Study of Former Canadian Participants of the Canada World Youth Program,* v. 4. Edmonton, Alberta, Canada: Canada World Youth. 1980.

Zimmerman, C. C. "Washington is Home". *Foreign Service Journal.* v. 47, n. 2. pp. 38-39; 45. 1970.

Part 3

**Intercultural Skills for
Corporate Cultural Systems**

A Case Study of a
Multicultural City: San Antonio
Henry Cisneros, Ph.D., Mayor of San Antonio

The Emergence of a Unique City

Like every other city, San Antonio is torn by the tugs, tensions and pulls of moder urban life, but we feel that in many respects we walk that urban tight-rope better than some. We are particularly proud of the city's ability to celebrate its culture, its charm, its legacy, its unique history, and to cement that in the physical manifestation of the city and in the daily lives of the people as we fulfill our ambition as one of the dynamic growing cities of modern America.

With respect to that legacy of the past, Will Rogers, the great American folklorist, once said that there were only four truly unique cities that he had visited in his travels around the United States. He said if someone put you on the streets of these cities with blindfolds on, then took the blindfolds off, you would quickly guess what city you were in. One city that met that test is Boston. Certainly Boston, with its revolutionary war flavor and New England heritage, is a unique American city. A second city he mentioned was San Francisco. If someone put you blindfolded in San Francisco and took the blindfolds off, and you saw the Golden Gate Bridge and had to dodge a cable car rushing by you, you would know you were in San Francisco. A third city that he mentioned was New Orleans. I've always had a suspicion that on a Saturday night in the French Quarter, even with blindfolds on, you could probably figure that you were in New Orleans. The fourth city that he mentioned was San Antonio, and I do believe that if someone put you on the River Walk and asked you to guess where you were, that you would have to say this could be no place but San Antonio.

San Antonio is a city rich in history, but the real story of our city today is twofold. First, it is a story of rapid growth and development in the model of the sunbelt cities: Phoenix, San Diego, Denver, Dallas, and Austin. San Antonio is among the most rapidly growing of the southwestern cities. Recently we had a meeting of the cities that John Naisbett, in his book *Megatrends,* called the ten cities of greatest opportunity in the years ahead. They were cities of Denver, San Jose, San Diego, Phoenix, Tucson, Albuquerque, Tampa, Salt Lake City, Austin, and San Antonio. There are interesting commonalities in the way-of-life in the southwestern cities and differences as compared to the cities of the northeast. I have lived in Boston and in Washington and have traveled throughout the northeastern United States and the central industrial belt in my duties as an officer of the National League of Cities. These cities of the southwest are more spreadout and newer; some of them did not even exist until after World War II. Phoenix didn't have a population of 100,000 until after World War II. Today it is the eighth largest city in the country and is to the computer, semi-conductor and micro-electronics industry what Detroit has been to automobiles.

Ethic of Intercultural Respect

The Hispanic community is large in every one of these "megatrend" cities and it creates a different dynamic for Hispanics than confronts other minority groups in other parts of the country. This is the second part of the story. The rising tide of the southwest lifts those who are coming to power with a dynamic force where two-plus-two-equals-five because of the lifting effect of economic and political power rising at the same time.

In San Antonio the accompanying theme to the notion of growth—both economic and political—is an ethic of respect for the Hispanic culture. San Antonio is the preeminent example of a city where consensus and dialogue, accommodation and cooperation, have become the bywords. With respect to the Hispanic community, this was not always so. As recently as fifteen years ago, San Antonio was characterized more as a city of division, a city of great hostility, a city where issues and basic questions of respect and representation at the City Council had not been resolved. The result was a city that could not address its longer-term problems because the fundamental front-burner issues had not been addressed. The legacy of that period remains with us. We remain a city that is very poor. It is one of the poorest cities in median income in the country, but we have put in place the building blocks that we think will result in great progress for the future.

Here, unlike Los Angeles where there are more Hispanics and Latin Americans, Hispanics are in positions of responsibility. In Los Angeles, for example, there is not one Hispanic on the Los Angeles City Council despite the fact that there are 800,000 Hispanics in the city. In San Antonio, we had the first Hispanic elected to United States Congress, Henry B. Gonzales, in 1961. Here, the first elected bishop, then archbishop, was named: Archbishop Patrick Flores, who I hope one day will be the first Hispanic cardinal; and we envision that that will be possible some day down the road. We have, if not a majority, at least a balance of Hispanics and whites on the City Council. In San Antonio, we have one of the most successful examples of community organization. The organization is called COPS, Communities Organized for Public Service, not built on parishes of the church, but on the Sol Alinsky model of the Industrial Areas Foundation. It has created an unprecedented focus for dialogue and consultation.

So, San Antonio is a laboratory case of intercultural respect historically and in the contemporary manifestations which are found on the street. We are not a city of large skyscrapers that come to the edge of the sidewalks thereby creating empty downtown streets and empty spaces after 5 o'clock, but instead a city that is referred to as a "city of human scale." Lower scale, warm textures, the River Walk, the area near the Convention Center, the Spanish Governor's Palace by the City Hall, and the Mercado—the Mexican market area—and the Fiesta Plaza, all contribute to the vitality of San Antonio. It is a safe environment, which is testimony to this respect for the history and legacy of the city. It is also a laboratory example where different cultures are attempting to work together in dealing with modern problems of governance.

International Trade and Investment

There are now an increasingly significant number of cities involved in what has previously been thought of as international models of cooperation. Cities in our country are engaging in international economic development, trade, investment decisions, and even foreign policy questions more than ever before. I would submit that in time some of the really interesting models that are developing in cities, as well as the cities that have been particularly adept, at these international issues should be studied. I cite some examples of how international cultural exchange and economic exchange are increasingly becoming the order of the day in cities.

The way to address this is to address different major topics, the first being trade. Cities more and more are conscious of the importance of international trade for their business. The mayor of Miami has established Miami as an effective financial capital of Latin America. First as a conference center, then as a financial center, Miami is playing an immensely important role in trade with Latin American countries. A city such as New Orleans, for example, has played a significant trade role historically and is once again stressing its relationship with the nations of the south. Los Angeles spends a great deal of time advancing its port, as do Long Beach and Seattle. The mayor of San Francisco is engaged in the same type of projection for the port facilities there. Phoenix, Arizona, not thought of as an international center, nevertheless has effectively persuaded local businesses to explore their export potential so that 60 percent of all local businesses can export products or services. In part, that environment was made more possible and more conducive by the existence of the foreign policy school in the Phoenix area.

More and more cities are engaged in trade. Mayor Young of Atlanta has walked away with the honors in this respect. By spending a great deal of time in Latin America, the Carribean and Africa, and by utilizing the entree that he gained as United States Ambassador to the United Nations, he has promoted Atlanta as an international city. He's been able to fashion contracts with countries in Africa, for example, that needed cable television, telecommunications and satellite hookups by serving as a liaison between those governments and Scientific Atlanta, a telecommunications company. Young has also helped the Saudi Arabians and other middle eastern nations in securing contracts for Atlanta companies. This is a role for cities that will be encountered in the years ahead.

A second dimension is that more and more cities are understanding the significance of investments in the United States. For example, as we run into instances of rising protectionism in the United States, the foreign nations, such as Japan, are recognizing that the way around protectionist legislation is to actually manufacture products—that they would usually import into the United States—within this country. There are eleven Japanese companies with major, thousand-person facilities in Tennessee. In addition, Yamasaki has recently moved a major Yamasaki tool works to Florence, Kentucky. Fujitsu has a plant in the Dallas area and Nippon Electric in northern California. Not only the Japanese, but also the Scandinavians are investing in biotechnology in northern New Jersey; and the Germans are investing in genetics and other biomedical facilities on the East Coast. Inland cities, such as Cincinnati, Ohio, have put a great deal of effort into relationships with the Germans, in particular.

Investment by foreign interests will require a greater understanding by the United States mayors, local officials, local universities and communities of this increasingly globalized economy with its globalized patterns of cross-investments. Those that understand language and cultural relationships and respect international cultures will have a greater stake in the future and be better off than those who continue to live in insular fashion.

Foreign Policy and Cultural Exchange

There are interesting relationships emerging at the local level in foreign policy as the global patterns just described result in foreign policy issues confronting the region, and cities and local areas. Such an international issue as immigration affects our daily lives in the southwest. The problems in Central America are another dimension that immediately impinge on and confront our way of life, particularly in the southwestern United States. I would submit that one of the great international trends for our country in the years ahead will be to learn about the issues that confront the nations to the south. For the better part of the 200 years of our nation's history we have given our best foreign policy face to the nations of the Atlantic Alliance. In the last 50 years, since the mid 1930's, our country has recognized the importance of the Pacific basin and indeed has had in the headlines of our nation's newspapers issues that relate to Japan, Korea, Vietnam, Philippines, Taiwan and China. That's appropriate in geopolitical terms.

Certainly the Pacific nations are critically important to our future, but never have we given our best face, our best diplomats, our best thinking or our best habits of respect to the countries that lie to the south. Yet these are nations that share the same land mass with us, not half-a-world away across an ocean, but across a bridge that can be walked. There are people from El Salvador in San Antonio, for example, who have walked here and people from Guatemala who walked across Mexico; not to mention the tens of thousands of undocumented workers fleeing economic conditions in Mexico. Not only are these nations on the same landmass, but they share a history. San Antonio was once part of the same nation as El

Salvador and Nicaragua. All were part of the Empire of Spain and later, Mexico. So, historically the ties are great. We are in the same time zone. We share the same Judeo-Christian religious base, not different religions in far flung places. Our interlaced history makes it imperative that our diplomacy and understandings of this part of the world take quantum leaps from where we are today.

If I learned anything in my service on the Kissinger Commission, the so-called Bipartisan Commission on Central America, it is that the problems of that part of the world are complex, urgent, timely and they cannot be swept away. If this generation of Americans chooses to respond to these issues by sweeping them under the rug and refusing to look at them, then certainly, the next generation of children will face problems that they will not be able to solve. We will hand them problems of revolution and bloodshed, famine, hunger and continued human suffering, if we choose not to make a major effort to begin to prepare our country to deal with these relationships. Who can better begin than Americans, who are by training and temperament prepared to deal with intercultural exchange?

San Antonio is playing the traditional roles that I have just described: trade, investment discussion, foreign trade zone, international air facilities, seminars in Mexico dealing with trade issues, and foreign policy relationships on immigration and Central American issues. We also have some nontraditional relationships. I recently opened an exhibit which is evidence of the intercultural climate in our city at the Instituto Mexicano. It is the only division of the Mexican Foreign Ministry which has a cultural institute as part of the cultural outreach of Mexico in a southwestern American city. It is an exhibit of the photographs of the Mexican Revolution, the late revolution and the 1900's to 1938 period of turmoil. It includes the periods of Mexico that saw Madero, Huerta, Carranza, Pancho Villa, and Zapata as the dominant figures on the Mexican scene. This preeminant photographer has an unbelievably valuable collection which is being shown on the walls of the Mexican Cultural Institute. The photographs are gripping in the way they capture the tension and drama of the Mexican Revolution. This is one example of cultural outreach matched with the University of Mexico. The only branch of UNAM, La Universidad Autonoma De Mexico, outside of Mexico is located here in San Antonio. Other nontraditional relationships which San Antonio has include the efforts of the Mexican American Cultural Center, which is a pastoral organization prepared to teach Latin American culture, the pastoral setting, language and theology to priests and nuns who are preparing to go into Latin American nations.

Mi Casa es Su Casa

Not only is San Antonio a city with a rich history, but it is also a place where the order of the day, the dominant ethic, is respect for other cultures. This is what Will Rogers referred to when he talked about ours being a unique city. This characteristic we celebrate as we continue to try to do something unique in a modern sense. We try to harness the best of what the American free enterprise system can offer and the best of what the American economy can generate. We do it in such a way that not only does it benefit those who have been outside the economic mainstream, but we do it in such a way that it is respectful of peoples' identities, cultures and dignity as they try to live in a multicultural setting in our beloved city of San Antonio.

In Spanish we say *"Mi casa es su casa,"* my home is your home. San Antonio is a new type of emerging multicultural arena. May it serve as a case study to advance our knowledge of better intercultural skills.

Multiculturalism and International Trade
Douglas Brannion

The topic of international trade demands attention to a number of factors. However, in this discussion, the approach is a highly practical one which explores examples and cultural "tips" for doing international trade.

International Trade and Culture Shock

A phenomenon which affects all of us in the Foreign Service and is not always well understood is culture shock. Even those of us who travel around the world on a continuous basis suffer from culture shock. It is a debilitating mental disease. One loses the day-by-day approach to decision making, fails to understand the other culture and has a tendency to sink into one's self. Instincts become suspect. One's actions, though perfectly justifiable in the Canadian context or in one's past experience, are inappropriate, and one's opinions and data base are irrelevant. In short, an identity crisis occurs. We feel persecuted, even unloved, and in our self-defense we want to lash out and knock this hostile environment into a shape we feel more at home in.

Not too many years ago in Indonesia my colleague went out to the airport, met a businessman and drove from the Jakarta airport. But, by the time they got to the motel, Michael realized something was wrong with this businessman. He thought the man was sick—probably from something he had eaten on the plane. Michael left him and said, "Ill be back to get you at seven for dinner at the house. We're having some people in."

We went back to the hotel at seven, but the man would not come out of his room. He said that there were all those funny people out there. He said, "I'm pushing my ticket under the door, you take it, get it reconfirmed, come back in the morning, you can take me to the airport." And that is what had to be done.

The Canadian government sends a lot of missions overseas. A few years ago they got the brilliant idea that there should not only be businessmen on these missions, but also labor representatives and academics. They had forgotten that the relationship in Canada between the labor unions and the business community traditionally has never been particularly close, though it is improving.

The Canadian Government launched one mission of high-priced executives and an executive of a labor union of electrical workers. Off they went into the Middle East. The labor union executive was a gentleman who had made the grand trip from Edmonton to Calgary, 170 miles, which represented his total experience outside of Edmonton. The man arrived in Beirut and went into shock. They sent him home because they knew he would not survive a stay in Iran.

In the Foreign Service, one has a longer time to adjust. But I think the prognosis for the disease of culture shock, if it is not handled properly, is terminal. For a cure, one has to undergo radical mental surgery. What is worse is that, one's family and colleagues are all suffering from the disease at the same time. They are moody and therefore augment one's persecution complex. The reaction of the Foreign Service employer, the Government, is an implied Darwinian ultimatum: Come home with your career and marriage in tatters, or adapt. So adapt, we must. The employer, of course, has laid the foundation for this Solomon-like choice by providing a two-minute psychological assessment prior to departure. As far as I can tell, this allows the employer to gamble that homicidal instincts will continue to be suppressed even under the torture of the culture shock.

As to psychological assessments, I remember almost 25 years ago, we were given 300 yes-no questions to answer in one hour. In addition, they gave us a Rorschach ink blot test. Unfortunately, I never see anything in those things. For a variety of reasons at that time, I did not want to be posted to Australia. However, I kept seeing maps of Australia. It worked! I have not been there yet, although now I would like to go to Australia. Except now my dog can not go and that is another cultural shock. Travelling around, families get attached to particular things and our 13 year old Shelty dog is ours. If that dog was not with my son when we went to another country, he would be very upset.

In the long run, the only choice for a Foreign Service Officer or anyone else faced with a cultural challenge is to adapt. This requires a monumental effort of good will in the first instance and a thick hide over a seemingly endless interval thereafter. To illustrate the point, let me cite a few cases. A colleague of mine was in Peru. He was invited by CIDA, which is the International Canadian Development Agency, to go in and open a project in the hinterland that the Canadian government had helped to fund. Miles felt it would be very useful to say a few words in Quechua. He began his speech with, according to his translation, a seemingly innocuous Quechua equivalent of the simple introduction, "Ladies and Gentlemen." The crowd burst into hysterical laughter and only later did he discover that he had used very graphic Quechua terms denoting the different sexes that are used to label toilets.

A different language is, of course, one of the first shocks we can encounter upon entering a different culture. If we do not understand the official at the airport when he or she asks for the passport, we are instantly in trouble, especially in some countries. But learning how to translate individual words is only part of the problem. Languages have the annoying habit of linking single words together, the sum of which can have an entirely different meaning. How does one explain the English expression "foothills" to a foreigner?

Another example of this concerns an American embassy official who had done very well with the language and was taking advanced Farsi training. One day his teacher corrected him, and instinctively he replied to what he had thought was a faultless translation into Persian or Farsi. "I'm sorry, I should have known that." The teacher simply smiled and said, "Very good, but what you have just said indelibly marks you as a foreigner. Modern Farsi is said to bar the word for sorry from Arabic. The Persians and the Arabs do not necessarily like one another, and a Persian never admits that he does not know something. What you should have said was, 'Thank you, I know that'."

In a different vein, I used to get in trouble when I was posted in Paris because I would always forget how to say, the English equivalent of "I am full." In vernacular French, however, that phrase conveys the somewhat surprising news that "I am pregnant." Language, as I have intimated, is one of the first indicators that we have entered a different culture. The same applies to dialect and even accent, as a Canadian traveling to Texas, and vice versa, will immediately acknowledge.

Practical Considerations
for Trade in Japan

Besides the United States, Canada's next largest trading partner, which purchases five per cent of our exports valued at approximately five billion dollars, is Japan. Since Japan is a different place to do business, I decided to concentrate on that country as an example of what businessmen had run into, when trying to do business and adjust to the culture.

Japan is not an easy market to enter and one needs all the assistance one can muster. It is a closed market except for raw materials.

We suggest that when planning a trip to Japan, you immediately get in touch with the Canadian Embassy. A large section of our foreign service is devoted to trade matters, and is available for assistance. In a particular country like Japan, we want people to get in touch with the foreign service because business calls cannot be made in Japan without a proper introduction. Japanese companies like to know ahead of time whom they are meeting and what organization is represented.

One will not necessarily meet the top management at first, for only middle management in Japan can recommend and initiate high level discussions. Key decision makers come in at a later stage of business dealings, but one might find later that they have been monitoring all of the proceedings. Be on time for the meetings and allow the whole day for them, as meetings can run a long time and may continue late into the evening. Often the meeting places are less spacious and less well appointed than we are used to in North America, but this should not cloud one's view. It is wise to be more formal than usual during a meeting. Have plenty of business cards on hand as there may be more people present than expected. I have yet to have a one-on-one official business visit of diplomacy with only one Japanese diplomat. There are always two and maybe even six diplomats. Business cards should be presented with the Japanese upwards. One will receive cards in return, which should be kept for reference. Do not write on them or mutilate them as this is a sign of disrespect. It is very useful to arrange them in front of one's self as a kind of a seating plan.

First meetings will probably begin with greetings and some general talk about Canada. The purpose of one's visit at this time will only be brought up later in the morning. The time is taken to get to know each other and to judge character and background. The North American business person will probably find someone with whom he/she can strike up a more personal relationship afterwards on a less formal level. This, of course, should be attempted and taken up with sincere good will, as this may prove to be just as important as the ceremonial meeting.

The Japanese, like their language, are traditionally evasive in a polite way and do not go in for the direct approach. It pays to be patient and to remain flexible as the Japanese are apt to do business on both logical and emotional levels. They are affected as much by the way of doing business as by the content. Strong sales pitches should not be given nor should provocative questions be asked in such a direct manner that they require unequivocal answers. They can easily be resented. Smoothness is all important, with strong opinions being expressed. From time to time there may be quiet periods when no one speaks. This does not indicate indifference; the silence should not be broken by off-the-cuff remarks or jokes among yourselves. Take time and adjust to the situation. Decisions in Japan are reached by consensus and by precedent. Once a decision is made, it is binding. Be alert to follow up on any interest showing.

Language is likely to be the single largest problem a North American will encounter in Japan. The number of Japanese people who speak fluent English is not great and knowledge of other foreign languages is extremely limited. In Tokyo and to a lesser extent in Osaka, a few people have an understanding of English, but outside these centers one is really on his/her own. Be sure to have explicit instructions written in Japanese before embarking on any trip, inside or outside of the cities. Do not expect to get by with a few words of Japanese if the going gets tough. It is a difficult language to use even in its elementary form.

As matters progress one will enjoy typical hospitality and to be well looked after by one's Japanese business associates. Do not expect to be invited into a Japanese home. Even among themselves, this is rarely done.

While the Japanese do not expect foreigners to understand the finer points of their etiquette, they appreciate it if the effort is made.

For example, it is not correct to walk on straw matting in a Japanese restaurant or home in shoes or slippers; these should be removed upon entering. Most Japanese meals are composed of a series of small dishes.

Naturally, it is polite to eat what is offered, but hosts are understanding if the foreign guests decline a particular dish such as raw fish. Incidentally, do not sit next to the host or the hostess because one is expected to sample everything. Once a foreigner says, "I really enjoyed that" he/she will get it again and again, and when eating a ten-course meal that can become difficult.

Japanese businessmen are enthusiastic golfers, and they may offer to arrange a game for foreign business contacts. A game of golf is an excellent way to cement a personal relationship in Japan. Green fees are high and courses are out of town. Allow plenty of time for travel, because there is no such thing as a quick game of golf in Japan.

It is not always necessary that hospitality is reciprocated at the time, but thanks must be extended. If one's Japanese acquaintances contact Business Canada, one has a chance to reciprocate. One meaningful way to say "thank you" would be to bring some typical souvenirs to Japan.

Here are some other guidelines for gift giving which are originally from the Parker Pen Company:

1. Let your Japanese counterpart initiate the gift exchange, unless he is visiting you or your gift is a reciprocation. It is not unusual to receive a gift when you first meet a Japanese businessman. It is not required that you immediately reciprocate with a gift. If you feel comfortable about one, however, it is wise to be prepared.

2. The return gift does not need to represent 100 per cent reciprocity. Thoughtfulness is more important. Do not expect the recipient of your gift to be effusive in his expression of appreciation. He may not even open it in front of you.

3. Present the gift when the recipient is alone unless you have a gift for everyone present.

4. Brand name items are appreciated in Japan.

5. Always bring a gift when visiting a home.

6. Do not open a gift in front of a Japanese counterpart, unless you ask if he would like you to do so. If he does not open your gift, your option is clear that you do likewise.

7. Do not surprise a Japanese person with a gift because he may be embarrassed by not having one for you at the moment.

8. Avoid ribbons and bows as part of the gift wrapping. Paper for wrapping signifies good taste.

In many ways the process of international trade in multicultural situations is a matter of how to do the process more than the content of negotiations. Perhaps in some way these sketches have provided a set of practical insights for skills.

European Consulting: A Perspective on Multiculturalism
Indrei Ratiu

Asking one European consultant to provide a perspective on multiculturalism is like asking a neighborhood storekeeper to tell you about the national retail industry, only worse. As far as I know, European consultants do not even have a common professional association. We have difficulty understanding one another, even when there is a common language. Sometimes there is not even that. A Flemish-speaking Belgian colleague confided in me the other day:

"I've been having a drink after work with someone lately, and it's really very strange. You see he is French-speaking.

"What do you mean?" I asked, wondering what was so strange about a 36 year old woman going out with a French-speaking fellow-countryman.

"I mean I have never really *discussed* things with a French-speaking Belgian before," she went on, "and when I told my husband, do you know what his reaction was? 'You're losing your culture', he said!"

From the United States side of the Atlantic it is probably hard to imagine that a sophisticated internal organization development consultant with a major multinational corporation could talk that way about her fellow countrymen, or that her husband should be so concerned about her culture. Her explanation was an eye-opener to me, too. This is symptomatic of the very local views we tend to have in Europe.

Given the difficulty any single European has in saying anything very meaningful about a European, let alone a multicultural perspective, (as with culture, I am part of the phenomenon itself), I shall state my own very limited qualifications to write on such a subject, to enable my own particular biases to be taken into account. If this first bit is overlong, please treat it as an intercultural experience; in France we really have to spell out the context before we can get to the point. Or treat it simply as one man's story of how he got to be in this rather unique profession.

Introduction and Background

First, let me outline my qualifications. I have a Romanian father and a British mother. I am no stranger on the U.S. side of the Atlantic since my parents maintain a home in Savannah, Georgia. I also have cousins from coast to coast who bear the same name. After Cambridge University, where I studied French and German, I embarked on a first career in journalism. I received an MBA at INSEAD (The European Institute of Business Administration, in Fontainbleau, France), and later did work toward my Ph.D. at the Business School in London. In the meantime, three to four years were spent running small companies; working on my Ph.D. (which I never completed) on crosscultural adjustment; comparing the learning strategies of international executives; and nearer to home, wondering why it was that my wife Iona (who is also Romanian) adjusted so well and I, seemingly, so badly on our various moves to different parts of Europe and trips around the world. My first consulting job was in the United States, designing multimedia financial training programs for the World Bank. At the same time, I was on the faculty of INSEAD, responsible for educational technology and executive development programs. It was also my first conscious professional concession to cultural differences: the faces on the slide show in the program were green. The interest in cultural differences grew as I turned increasingly to consulting in management development with a small number of multinational corporations in Europe. Much of this was training. I puzzled over why we would talk endlessly over drinks and meals about cultural differences, without a word on the subject in the formal part of the program. For Maslow, Herzberg, McClelland and Berne, it seemed that the only mention of cultural differences were those that supported their own view of motivation or personality. And yet, very politely, people in courses seemed to be saying: "These ideas are all very interesting, but there is more to it than this." I took to searching for management research which was directed against the popular view of the time. This was that technologies and, therefore, values and beliefs were converging throughout the world.

Back in the seventies, an American INSEAD faculty member named Jim Stevens, used to give the same case of interdepartmental conflict to small national groups of American, British, French and

German managers. Over time, some interesting patterns emerged: The French would conclude that the answer to the problem was to escalate, to give it to higher management to resolve. The Germans would say, "Work out systems and procedures to resolve this, and don't rock the boat." The British would talk about the need for negotiations and better communications, and the Americans would discuss the need for greater sensitivity and trust.

Stevens' work inspired some massive European research projects by André Laurent (1983) in France and Geert Hofstede (1980) in Holland which, together with work by John Childs (1981) in the UK, has documented the thesis that if technologies are converging, managerial values are, if anything, diverging. Laurent, in particular, found that people from the same multinational organization (i.e., same technology) are marginally more likely to disagree along cultural lines than if they come from different organizations. This work has been nicely reviewed by Nancy Adler (1985) in her book *International Dimensions of Organizational Behavior.*

These developments have also inspired three independent consultants, based in Paris (from France, the UK and the US, of which I was one), to work on the dynamics of multicultural management teams not only with their clients, but also by being a practicing multicultural management team themselves. We started in the winter of 1982-83. Business has now developed to the point where the team also has Dutch, French-Canadian, Japanese, and Spanish members. When we first started, people said we were crazy. French friends asked: "Culture is socialism, and you're aiming at business?" Contacts in international organizations said: "We're all international civil servants here. We are supposed to have left our cultural differences behind. It's a subject we don't like talking about." This was just about the time UNESCO was first coming under fire from certain parts of the world for both mismanagement and devaluing its founders' noble ideas. This cultural conflict quickly turned into a political conflict between a "Doing" versus a "Being" concept of what an international cultural organization should actually be about. British friends meanwhile said: "Interesting, but we're not sure we really need you. After all we've been at this game a long time." In Germany, SIETAR International member Stefan Wirtz bravely launched a public seminar on intercultural issues for management. Unfortunately, this had to be cancelled when a sudden economic downturn raised other more pressing priorities for the business community in Germany.

Anyway, we started. Curiously, it was within just two private sector companies, reputed to have particularly strong *corporate* cultures, that our own interculturally oriented consultancy first got off the ground. This was quite a surprise to us. The only other wholly interculturally oriented consultancy that we know of in Europe is currently Jean Phillips-Martinsson's Cross-Cultural Relations Center in Stockholm, Sweden. We are not exactly talking about a current major industry, but rather one with potential.

The focus of these small European consultancies is very different from what it is in the United States. Briefing is relatively unimportant. Cross cultural communications training and what Stephen Rhinesmith and I are calling multicultural Organization Development (OD) seem much more relevant to the European situation. The differences are there for all to see, and we Europeans are perhaps not particularly interested in intra-European briefing because we do not actually think those differences are going to be all that important. After all, we drive on one another's roads, eat one anothers' food, share a Common Market. It comes to most of us in Europe as something of a shock to discover how far apart we are on such basic questions as how to entertain a dinner guest or write a business letter, let alone on how to run a meeting or how to organize for results. Also, virtually every European country already has its own, "Briefing Center," usually with government support, which has for decades provided preparation for people going further afield than Europe, typically to former colonies. A number of SIETAR International members are affiliated with such organizations: Jacques Foubert is the Director of the CFECTI in France, Patrick Lloyd is the Director of the Farnham Castle Centre for International Briefing in the UK, Pete van der Kleut is with the Royal Tropical Institute of the Netherlands, and Dieter Clajus is with the Bad Honnef Briefing Center in West Germany. Working more at the community level, every country also has a vast network of typically not-for-profit associations providing education, counselling and information facilities relating to the growing ethnic minorities and the young. It is this last group, incidentally, which probably mobilizes the largest number of people interested in intercultural issues in Europe, and which is the least represented in SIETAR International's current membership in Europe. Roberto Ruffino, of Intercultura and EFIL, the European Federation for Intercultural Learning, addresses the youth part of this area in another chapter of this book.

My own perspective is very much from the business end of the consulting spectrum. At InterCultural Management Associates (ICM) we make efforts to keep abreast of developments in other parts of the field by our membership in SIETAR France and by initiating and producing a world directory of institutions involved in intercultural studies, with SIETAR International's help. This is the so-called *UNESCO Directory* because it draws on the central database and publication facilities of UNESCO.

Major Trends and Implications for European Consultants

What are the major trends in European consultancy today and what implications can be drawn for consultants working from an intercultural perspective? I want to draw on the Euro-American perspective of Bill Ouchi (1980), known for his Theory Z in the US, and Paul Evans (1984), known for his work on the personal costs of executive success in Europe.

Ouchi and Evans, drawing on earlier work at the University of Pennsylvania by the industrial economist Oscar Williamson, describe organizations in terms of bureaucracies, markets and clans. Bureaucracies are basically about equity, or how to maintain smooth internal functioning in a hierarchically structured organization. Markets are about performance, or how to improve operating results. And clans, somewhat surprisingly perhaps, are about innovation and flexibility, or how to achieve results in the longer term under conditions of uncertainty. Ouchi and Evans' basic point is that Human Resources Management's strategic dilemmas and orientations can usefully be described using these labels. I want to use these labels to address the changes we have been witnessing in Europe and some of the questions these changes raise for us as interculturally-oriented consultants.

If we train our view on Europe as a whole as opposed to individual countries or the strategic orientation of individual boards, I believe we are currently witnessing a bigger shift in orientation than any I have personally seen in the fifteen years since I first became involved with business. It is a shift to a concern for performance and productivity, on the one hand, and for innovation and flexibility, on the other hand; and away from the equity dimension.

In much of Europe, particularly in the more southern parts, we are relatively high on what Geert Hofstede (1980) calls "power-distance"; that is to say we accept the fact that power is distributed pretty unequally in our organizations. Until very recently, when the equity dimension was in fashion, demand was high for communications oriented programs that, frankly, were about making people happier with the status-quo in the organization, even if the titles were "Creativity," "Communications" and the like. In France, for instance, we have a law (the *Loi Auroux*) that obliges managements to organize sessions in which personnel can "express themselves." Under an equity orientation, people are particularly concerned with improvements in working conditions and self-expression. Consultants like Hay, who specialize in systematic job grading, are much in demand because they basically sell a system that maintains equity in a hierarchical or unequal situation.

From our own perspective, there seems to have been a European-wide shift away from these kinds of equity preoccupations. People are talking either "results," which is the language of performance of the "market" type organization; or "corporate culture," which is the language of innovation and flexibility of the "clan" type of organization. That does not mean that equity oriented interventions are no longer called for: the basic Hay job grading service is still a very big business. But it does mean that it is difficult to start out in Europe at present without taking account of this major shift. Offerings on "A Synthesis of Eastern and Western Philosophy for Management" are not exactly in demand. (But the Japanese game of "Go" is currently fashionable in management circles in France, no doubt because of its very precise lessons for strategy implementation).

Interestingly, this shift seems to be European-wide, and beyond, irrespective of government policy. Recently, our colleagues, Middle East Industrial Relations Consultants in Athens, held their annual conference for human resource managers in the Arab World. It was entitled: "Human Resource Management in the Arab World—the Crucial Issues." The crucial issue was. . .*productivity*! In Northern Europe you might well expect the centerright governments in Scandinavia, West Germany, the Netherlands and the UK to have provided a framework for such a shift. But strangely, even the left-leaning governments in Spain, France and Italy have provided an ideological and, to some extent, a legislative context within which profitability is no longer considered a dirty word. Even Mr. Gorbachev is going for results rather than equity these days. At ICM we recently had a visitor from the University of Lodz in Poland, a professed member of Solidarity, who is researching corporate culture shifts from bureaucracy to performance, and consulting (on a private basis) to Polish enterprise on how to make such changes work. The reason why this is possible, he explained, is that, whatever Poles' feelings may be about the present regime, there is at least a basic consensus around the need for a shift away from excessive bureaucratization in Polish organizations.

For consultants to business and industry working in the intercultural field, we believe this shift away from equity towards performance, innovation, and flexibility opens up major responsibilities for researching and articulating the impact of what we do as consultants. And this, I believe, will also contribute to the ongoing discussion about ethics within SIETAR International, as well as promote better service to our clients (for those of us who are professionally active as consultants).

For example, we need to be able to state why good cross-cultural communications are important in business as well as social terms. What is it that good cross-cultural communications can contribute to improving operating results?

What do we know about the dynamics of cultural changes in both nationally as well as internationally operating organizations? For example, what do we know about the dynamics of cultural change that can assist management in start-ups, spin-offs, mergers, acquisitions and team building? I believe that collectively in organizations like SIETAR International and within major corporations, a lot is known about these issues. The problem is simply that, in spite of the valiant efforts of such publishers as SIETAR International; the Intercultural Press; the International Consultants Foundation; ASTD which recently launched the *International Human Resource Development Annual*; Elsevier, which recently launched the *Journal of Management Consulting;* Sharpe with the *International Studies of Management and Organization*; and Pergammon, Sage, Gulf and Hogrefe, all of which have intercultural collections, many consultants have not as yet done a very good job of pulling together the pieces that we *do* know.

Questions Applied to
Intercultural Management

I would like to mention a few ideas around these questions, drawn from our own practice in ICM (InterCultural Management Associates). On the question of what good cross-cultural communications can contribute to operating results, the cost of premature return of an expatriate family is by now well-documented, but European management is still waiting to be convinced. There is also the idea that performance, along with innovation and flexibility in multiculturally staffed organizations, has something to do with an over-riding corporate culture that can integrate a wide range of diversity. How many readily identifiable corporate cultures can you think of that are multiculturally staffed and do *not* have some degree of recognition of cultural differences in the human resource development area? Royal/Dutch, ITT, Phillips, IBM, Schlumberger, British American Tobacco all give recognition to cultural differences, *within* a readily identifiable, over-riding corporate culture. Although they are multiculturally staffed, you are not likely to find cultural differences on the program in either UNESCO or the Secretariat of the EEC. Neither of these two public institutions are particularly noted for their over-riding corporate cultures or for their performance. Instead, their role is promoting an elusive consensus.

I am deliberately exaggerating the contrast here because I do not really know how this relationship between recognizing cultural difference, an overriding corporate culture, and the dimensions of performance, innovation and flexibility actually functions. But intuitively, it makes sense, doesn't it? If cultural differences are seen as posing a threat to the cohesiveness of culture of the organization, they are not going to be publically emphasized. We need more data on this relationship.

As background from our own intercultural literature, I can think of a persuasive essay by Frantz Fanon (1965) "On National Culture," which relates cultural flowering, or performance, to a concept of nationhood that can override ethnicity and provide a framework within which people of all kinds can contribute to the common good. There is also a wealth of sociological and anthropological literature on the making of this great nation that could also provide us with valuable insights into what is required to develop unity with diversity in the corporate sphere. Alternatively, if management looks to innovation and flexibility for long-term improvements in the bottom-line, and if these characteristics are indeed to be found in organizations whose staff see themselves as members of the "clan" or "extended family," then we, as consultants with an intercultural perspective, can immediately connect with the significance of cultural symbolism, or of "clan get-togethers," where the high-context, informal rule systems identified by Edward Hall (1977) are able to develop. In terms of our practice as consultants with an intercultural perspective, it means that we should start thinking very carefully, with our clients, about the nature of this relationship between corporate culture; cultural difference; and performance, innovation and flexibility when considering multicultural environments.

On my second question regarding the dynamics of cultural change, much of our recent work in ICM has been specifically concerned with the dynamics of cultural shifts from a primary concern with the equity dimension towards either (or both) the performance or innovation and flexibility dimensions in multicultural environments. In such environments, we have been struck by the tremendous potential of a well-defined task to produce high levels of motivation, provided there is relative freedom and support for local culture groups to define how to implement. Here are some examples of what I mean by the word "task" in this context. Let's say the task is "to manage by objectives." I now believe you would be hard put to find a manager anywhere who would have any difficulty with that. The problems start when going a step further and saying: "and our approach to managing by objectives is. . ." and one wheels out John Humble from the UK, Blake and Mouton's Management Grid, or some other ready-made approach or model. Similarly with performance appraisal: let us say the task is "to appraise performance." It is by recommending a certain *way* of appraising performance that we run into difficulties. BAT Industries have different approaches to performance appraisal throughout the world. Group management simply says: "you will appraise performance. *How* you do it is up to you." Or let us say that a business is taking measurements in oilwells. The task is defined very precisely in terms of quality, safety and service. Contrary to what I myself used to believe, however, it does not really matter, in performance terms, if off the job the Malays, Nigerians and Scandinavians do not mix. This is something I learned not only with a client but from our own organization as well. When members of the team get together socially (Dutch, French, Spanish, Japanese, British, American), the only common threads we have are related to the work we do. If we choose to really *relax*, we would much sooner be with our own folk.

This is controversial material perhaps precisely because so much work on cross-cultural communications has been done within the framework of the American melting-pot ideal. Geert Hofstede's (1980) work is particularly illuminating here, where he shows that it is highly individualistic societies that tend to universalize with respect to their values and beliefs. In the corporate sphere this means that those of us from the US, UK and Australia actually feel more comfortable with people in our corporations who share our beliefs, while those of us from more collectivistic societies feel more comfortable with people in our corporations who are loyal. I remember the public controversy in Britain in the seventies over whether Sikh public transportation staff should be obliged to wear company caps or not, in the interest not so much of corporate identity, but allegedly of such values as safety, hygiene, etc. And I compare that with the manning arrangements I saw in the multilingual, multiculturally staffed cotton-mills in Ahmedabad. The local Indian production supervisor seemed to me at that time to be very tough indeed. But all he was really doing was spelling out the task very clearly and demanding absolute loyalty. He did not tread the delicate ground of values other than with respect to the minimum required to get the job done. That minimum included standards of safety and hygiene, but only those that were narrowly task related.

The implications for cultural change and more narrowly also for technology transfer are important. In our own work at ICM we find ourselves distinguishing very carefully, in both cultural change and technology transfer situations, between, on the one hand, *what* needs to be done, and, on the other hand, *how* to go about it. The *what* is the non-negotiable part: that "safety to certain standards will be ensured," or that "performance will be appraised as a basis for management development," or that "European-level decisions will be implemented in the following areas." *How* (in other words, by what means) performance appraisals, safety standards, European level decisions are actually implemented in a second culture becomes an issue for negotiation. This is where we find culturally sensitive consulting support is particularly called for so that local teams can satisfy company requirements within the context of local values.

What sorts of sources should we turn towards to guide us in this kind of work? Remember that the key words along the performance dimension are "markets" and "teams," words which give us plenty of clues on how to proceed in ways appropriate to local "team" values. There is also, I understand, literature on the "cultures" of teams: the need for discipline, keeping the score, regular feedback, or heroes to emulate. The key words along the flexibility and innovation dimension have to do with "clans," "extended families," long-term development, and symbolism, which give us clues to which I have already referred. With respect to the dynamics of culture in start-ups, spin-offs, mergers and acquisitions, Geert Hofstede's work (1980) and on-going research is a particularly valuable resource. Why, for example, have the corporate marriages behind Unilever and Royal Dutch/Shell been such successes, and the Dunlop/Pirelli and VFW/Focker link-ups such flops? What makes Airbus Industrie work, while the Common Market, in many areas, flounders? At least part of the story is "cultural compatibility." Hofstede shows how very compatible, in cultural terms, are Dutch and British values (Unilever and Royal Dutch/Shell), and how relatively incompatible, in comparison, are Dutch/German (VFW/Focker) and British/Italian (Dunlop/Pirelli) combinations. As in the marriage market, this sort of data does not mean that management teams should not necessarily try. Such research merely highlights the shoals to watch out for when attempts are made. Here too we consultants have our part to play.

In this short tour of the horizon of European consulting from an intercultural perspective I seem to have focused more on the macro rather than the micro aspects of our field. The reason is perhaps that the micro level of intercultural communications is itself more a feature of the equity dimension—how to maintain the smooth internal functioning of a hierarchically organized, multicultural society. In Europe that seems to be a major concern within society at large, but not, I believe, within our major corporations, where performance, innovation and flexibility seem to be the current preoccupations. It is these preoccupations that call on our skills not only as intercultural communications specialists, but as dynamically oriented cross-cultural anthropologists, concerned with the macro issues of culture and cultural change.

I have referred very little to organization development. This is because, working *within* a multicultural team on the kinds of issues that multicultural teams face in organizations, we in ICM have come to see the intervention techniques traditionally associated with organization development as limited to a relatively narrow range of organizational experience—that of the English-speaking world. Outside that world we need broader frameworks, both for analysis and for intervention. Here I have proposed Ouchi (1980) and Evans (1984), and Hofstede (1980) as useful schemes for the purposes of analysis. For the purposes of intervention I have presented two simple concepts that we, in ICM, are finding particularly useful in our work with multiculturally staffed clients: the concept of task definition and the concept of an overriding corporate culture within which collective cultural differences can be recognized. To find out more about these limitations of traditional Organization Development, other information will, hopefully, be available after more observations and future work.

References

Adler, Nancy. *International Dimensions of Organizational Behavior*. Boston, MA: Kent Publishing Co. 1985.

Child, John. "Culture, Contingency and Capitalism in the Cross-national Study of Organizations." In L.L. Cummings and B.M. Staw, eds. *Research in Organizational Behavior*, v. 3. 1981.

Evans, Paul. "On the Importance of Generalist Conception of Human Resource Management: A Cross-national Look." *Human Resource Management*. v. 23, n. 4. 1984.

Fanon, Frantz. "On National Culture." *The Wretched of the Earth*. Harmondsworth, UK: Penguin Books. 1965.

Hall, Edward. *Beyond Culture*. New York: Anchor Books. 1977.

Hofstede, Geert. *Culture's Consequences: International Differences in Work Related Values*. Beverly Hills, CA: Sage Publications. 1980.

Laurent, André. "The Cultural Diversity of Western Conceptions of Management." *International Studies of Management and Organisation*. v. XIII, n. 1-2. 1983.

Ouchi, W.G. "Markets, Bureaucracies and Clans." *Administrative Science Quarterly*, v. 25. 1980.

Addresses of Resources
Mentioned in the Text

American Society of Training and Development, 1630 Duke St., P.O. Box 1443, Alexandria, VA 22313, USA.

Elsevier Science Publishers. P.O. Box 1991, 1000 BZ, Amsterdam, The Netherlands.

Gulf Publishing. P.O. Box 2608, Houston, TX 77001, USA.

Hogrefe International, Inc., P.O. Box 51, Lewiston, NY 14092, USA.

The Intercultural Press, Box 768, Yarmouth, ME 04097, USA.

The International Consultants Foundation, 11612 Georgetowne Court, Potomac, MD 20854, USA.

Pergammon Press, Headington Hill Hall, Oxford OX3 OBW, UK and Fairview Park, Elmsford, New York 10523, USA.

Sage Publications, 28 Banner St., London EC1Y 8QE, UK and 275 South Beverly Dr., Beverly Hills, CA 90212, USA.

M. E. Sharpe, Inc., 80 Business Park Dr., Armonk, New York, NY 10504, USA.

SIETAR International, 1505 Twenty-Second St., N.W., Washington, DC 20037, USA.

Part 4

**Intercultural Skills for
Macro-Cultural Systems**

The Media and Multicultural Societies*
Samuel Betances, Ph.D.

The Media as Shaper of Cultural Vision

The media names and symbols in multicultural settings, both the good and the bad, are influential. I will discuss the media and put it within the framework and the context of a multicultural setting.

Over the last few years it has been my privilege to travel and to see different parts of the world. So not only do I know some things intellectually, but I have also experienced them. I have been to Japan four times in the past year and a half. Japan is interesting because we are able to see a really homogeneous society at work, at play, in the market place, in politics, at worship and in the media. It is interesting to realize that when you take a look at what the media often reports about Japan, it assumes that there are lessons that can be transplanted to a heterogeneous, multicultural society such as ours and that somehow we stand to benefit from that situation. It dawned on me that we have here something very unique, something very different.

There is a consensus of sort in Japan. It does not mean that Japan does not have minorities and people who are subordinated. What it means is that usually the framework of Japan cannot be generalized when comparing it to the United States. When I realized that young women can walk in a city with more than ten million people without fear of being assaulted; when I went into the Genza district I realized that there was a place to put my umbrella before I went into the store and when I came back it would still be there; when I realized that if I forgot my camera the taxi drivers would do everything possible to return it; I realized that this is a unique situation. I saw a woman dressed for success and as I saw her I asked my guide, Micca, the person to whom I go when I am in Tokyo—A Chicano from East Los Angeles—"Why is she wearing that?"

Mica looked and said, "I do not understand."

"Why is she wearing that? Look again."

He said, "I do not understand."

I said, "The mask, the surgical mask."

"Oh, you see, she has a cold and it's her responsibility not to infect other people." So it was understood that this was part of her cultural baggage within the framework of this particular culture, the individual is responsive to the group.

In Yoyigo Park by Olympic Stadium I saw young people who dance. They dressed themselves almost like what we see in American movies and in the images of gangs on the media. But, on the back of their jackets they had written in English, "bad son of good family." The worst that a Japanese young person could say is that they are not in harmony with the family. That was the ultimate act of rebellion and they chose English in which to say it.

I have traveled to Germany, Costa Rica, Israel, and several times to Mexico and Canada. By comparison, it seems to me that one of the things that we must understand about the United States is it is different in the sense that there are people from all over the world who are here either for voluntary or involuntary reasons, and they call this nation their home. Israel is also a multicultural society, but is one fifth the size of California. When I think of the multicultural nation, I think of the people who visit Chicago as a great American city, but Chicago is also a great Polish city. This country has more black people than there are people in Australia, than there are people in Canada, than there are people in Portugal. The United States, it is said, is either the fourth or the fifth largest Spanish-speaking country in the world. We have people who are Americans, but who are also Scandinavian in decent. In the United States we have people from all kinds of places, from Asia and from the Islands of the Pacific, the Samoans and Chamoros. We have people who basically come to this country to settle in the land of people who were immigrants. The British, after all, were also settlers. The priests transplanted their institutions. They did not migrate into what was established, but replaced, took back, and pushed back.

The vision we get from the media is interesting. So much is said about the Holocaust and there ought to be more said for we must never forget what happened. Keep in mind, however, that Hitler, through the Nazi control of that empire, was able to get rid of sixty per cent of the people called Jews; while our ancestors, those who were called Americans, eliminated seventy-five per cent of the people we called Indians! The difference is that in Germany there is no romanticizing that fact. There are no statues celebrating the fact of Nazism, but not an evening goes by without some western movie recycling the notion of savages, of cowboys, and of Indians. Thus, what happens to differences in the United States is not so much that they exist, but the meaning that we have given to those differences has changed. The media contributes to that condition.

We find that human beings have a great capacity to give meaning to physical objects as well as animated ones. We can take a piece of cloth and say it is a handkerchief and give it a function. The meaning is not in the cloth. It's in the culture, because you can take the same piece of cloth, make it a blouse and give it the function of both protecting and celebrating you. You could take that piece of cloth and declare it to be a towel and you will dry your body with it or lay on it on the beach. Or you can take that piece of cloth and you can declare it a flag as the signature of peoplehood symbolizing the people's identity and nationality. One is willing to die for it, as we celebrate in the symbol of Hiroshima. Basically, in a piece of cloth we invest emotions. Through that piece of cloth we create symbolism that brings out either outrage, scandal or an oath.

In that sense, the difference that "differences" make in the United States of America is that for too long we have put meaning not on cloth, but on the perception of physical characteristics such as color, hair texture, gender, age, religion, language competencies and social class. We have decided to regulate people to be the handkerchiefs of life, to be the blouses and towels. Yet, we have secured a prominent place for those whom we would celebrate to be flags. I submit to you that this nation is not only a multicultural nation, but it is also a nation in conflict with its values. We have found that the meaning is not in the cloth; the meaning is not in the gender; the meaning is not in the hair; the meaning is in the culture.

If there is one job that we must do—that must supersede our consultant work, that must be expressed in our research, that must be our preoccupation—it is understanding the impact of the negative meaning that has been given to all of God's children on earth. The superior dominant forces have defined those who are basically relegated to inferior social roles. So, I submit to you that what we have here is not so much the media in multicultural settings, but rather how those multicultural settings continue to maintain stereotypes, to dehumanize and to make less of human beings. I submit to you that we must look at that reality closely as we consider the good and the bad in media.

The media in the United States has for too long presented a homogeneous value system in a heterogeneous reality. So, the problem of American society is the definition of what makes an American. It is a challenge that almost every generation in the United States has to confront. The definition of American women is changing as women realize that for too long sexism somehow meant that women were denied access to wealth, power and prestige. A series of explanations for sexism were given that blamed the victims. What women have to confront is that they are no longer satisfied with being the handkerchiefs and towels of life.

Media as Shaper of Cultural Life

The media, especially television, are relative newcomers in our lives, but the media have tremendous power. You cannot pick up an introductory sociology book or enter the world of education without realizing that one of the shapers of the vision that we have about ourselves, about our society, and about our place in the world comes from media. The media have joined important agencies of socialization, of civilizing people into adulthood, as have the family, the church and education. In fact, by the time a young person reaches the age of fifteen, he or she has watched seventeen thousand hours of television and has heard twenty thousand hours of radio. Yet, he or she has only experienced eleven thousand hours of basic school and three thousand hours of teaching in the church! More than the church and the school combined, television and radio reach into the minds and the spirits of our young people through cartoons, entertainment, films, sports events and music. We must understand clearly that the media shapes individuals in ways that the individuals are not really aware that they have been shaped.

I remember as a young person in New York City I used to watch a television program called "77 Sunset Strip". It was entertaining. (By the way, I have enjoyed television. I've grown up with it. I have television sets in my home. I'm not anti-television. I love it. Not only that, but I've made part of my living on it.) I remember the images that television portrayed in "77 Sunset Strip". There was an actor by the name of Ed Burns who was called Cookie. The theme song was "Cookie, Cookie, loan me your comb." Burns would take out a comb and begin to comb from one end to the other. It was a thin comb and I used to look at the hair and say, "I wish I had hair like that. I wish I could do that." You see, if I attempted to do that my comb would not reach the other side with all of its teeth! The message we got was that "blonds have more fun."

Basically, when we saw "Father Knows Best" and "Ozzie and Harriet" and all of these shows, we knew we did not belong. It was not because Ozzie and Harriet had said, "We want to make a statement that dark skinned Hispanics from mixed marriages have bad hair." Nothing like that. I knew I had *pelo malo* (bad hair). Because I wanted to have good hair, I used to take one of my mother's stockings, cut it and make a cap. Then I cut my hair real short and took all of the products that come out of image-making and put on that cap and slept head up. The next day I would take it off and there was a little mark around the back of my head. But let me tell you, I did all this because I wanted to be like the images I saw.

Something remarkable has happened to this nation because black folks started something. Black folks started with a very simple idea. They started with the idea that black was beautiful. This did not mean that white was ugly. It just meant that it was different. It meant that Blacks began to reject rejection, not themselves. Black folks no longer needed to cook their hair; brown folks no longer needed to hide in the shadows of bus stop signs to keep from getting darker; and some of us who are brown and dark did not necessarily have to marry lighter skin people than ourselves. Some of us began to realize that if we are good enough for God, we ought to be good enough for the United States of America. Is it not wonderful to realize that we are beautiful not despite our brownness, not despite our blackness, but because of it?

Would you believe that there was a time when I actually thought that I was ugly? I realized that my image could not come from the media because my image would be of Alan Ladd and Marilyn Monroe. Even when you think of the novels that come out of Mexico, Chile, Venezuela and Puerto Rico (which were for some reason buried in history) we have the same patterns, for the same reasons emerging in different ways. Thus, what we have to realize is that we did not have the power to change the media.

The media practiced an interesting way of looking at things. The media taught us in subtle ways. The media would not give us programs in prime time that reflected the goodness, the intelligence, the compassion, our loyalty, our struggles and our triumphs. Basically, the media made us less loyal, less committed to democracy and, in a way, more violent and lazier than what we really were. What we have to do is to begin to reject rejection. Also, if we inherited the homogeneous values that came through the media and we internalized those things, we would not be able to be our own best friends. We would choose to be like so and so and it would never occur to us that what we really had to be was the way we are, in the way that God made us.

I remember as a child going to a place called Coney Island. At this amusement park, there were mirrors. You would look at yourself through those mirrors and laugh because you looked very little, very fat, very tall or very skinny. Those were mirrors of distortion. You laughed because you knew that. What about our young people when they see themselves through the eyes of their teachers, when they see themselves through the distorted image of one dimensional thinking and knowing? What then?

Every time a policeman or private eye captured, reformed or killed the criminal in a detective story, according to Dr. McDonald, he was communicating the message that crime does not pay. Every time a boy met a girl, lost her, then regained her, the program promoted the importance of personal fulfillment in romantic love. Inherent in every religious broadcast was the endorsements of freedom of religion. Whenever a child on T.V. follows the command of an adult, the show communicates the validity of obedience to the youngster. Even news programs had an American slant focusing primarily upon what transpired at home, be it at the local, town, state or national level or upon external matters impacting upon the United States. Basically, since the established political order wanted stability, television was a reflection of that, and as a consequence, inherently political. Therefore, if some of us wanted to see things change and were willing to confront the system, we were viewed as problematic. Thus, I found it interesting that when black folks—during the Civil Rights Movement—began to demand a proper reflection of their hopes and aspirations within the framework of what America had preached, there was no place in prime time television for blacks except as baboons. In fact, there were two programs in prime time television which featured dogs as central characters, "Lassie" and "Rin Tin Tin", but not one program that reflected the black experience in positive ways. Doesn't the sense of the media, the goodness of the media, the excellence of the media, the technology of the media assume that only certain people could personalize and universalize the human condtion? So it was that only "The Little House on the Prairie" could reflect what the family was all about; it never occurred to them that the Cosby Show about a Black family could find acceptance.

It was assumed that some of us could entertain America at our expense, at the expense of our group. What could you tell our young inspired actors and actresses? The fact of the matter is that you have to get there before you can say, "no." But, in order for you to get there you have to say, "yes," to a lot of compromises. What kind of advice do you give people in the media in international settings about the way they reflect their minorities, their subordinate groups in their society? Do you merely visit developing nations and figure out ways by which they can get the American prime time shows and how they can translate them into their language? Or do you provide some compassion as well?

Its interesting to me that my political hero, Jack Kennedy, was responsible for sending the man by the name of Solomon to Micronesia, to the less-developed islands of the Pacific. One of the recommendations he made was to use television as the small islands prepared themselves for self-determination. American television would develop an American bias when the time comes for their making a choice. They would favor America, although not necessarily in their best interest.

I went to Saipan in the Mariana Islands and found that television had done its work, and radios had done their work. The Chamoros knew that their island really belonged to the Americans; the Carolinians did not have much to say about it. They are bicultural island nations that are very small in numbers, but total societies nevertheless. I was giving a lecture because I work in this arena of the non-material aspects of development. I thought I would communicate what I wanted to say by asking them how important holidays were to them. Ninety-nine per cent of all the monuments in the Marianas are for the Spanish, the Germans, the Japanese, and the Americans, not for the people of the islands. That is the image that they are getting. So, I took a look and we talked about the significance of a flag as an image of the people. I looked at the flag.

There was the ladestone, there was the blue, there was the star. I began to analyze the significance of the flag: the blue is the ocean, the ladestone is the continuity of peoplehood and the culture of the Chamoros, and the star was part of the United States by treaty. I said, "And where are the Carolinians?" "Oh, no we forgot the Carolinians!"

In their haste to imitate the symbolism which they have seen, they had not internalized the responsibility that they had to all of the people of the land. Were you a consultant, were you a Peace Corps volunteer, were you an advisor, would you suggest how to make a flag that did not reflect the aspirations? I recently learned there is a law now in place which directs that there be a revision of the Micronesian flag to include the Carolinians.

The media can create striking changes in a people, just as the media can create a self-image of those same people in the first place. Through symbols and imagery we are shaped. Let us continue to be informed and aware of the hold of the media in multicultural societies.

* Edited from a taped transcription

The State of Intercultural Education Today

Beulah F. Rohrlich, Ph.D.

Anyone interested in writing on intercultural education does so as a labor of love. Without a fixed body of literature, a clear pattern of origin and history or key names from which to trace developments, we are like people trying to climb a mountain with no trails. We know the mountain exists because we're on it. We know it has a summit, and we think we can reach it by drawing from past knowledge and by sharing with our companions plans and methods. We are a small group facing a challenge, and the rest of the world seems relatively unconcerned with what we consider important or with the outcome of our endeavors.

This chapter is a modest attempt to place in perspective what is meant by intercultural education in the United States by someone who has taught intercultural education for the past ten years, and has had contact with related disciplines on a university campus and with community projects involving practical applications. Within these pages we will focus on terminology, historical perspectives, notable contributions, guidelines from practitioners and suggestions for the future. Like most people teaching intercultural communication, this writer considers herself an educator only in the broadest sense of the word, but not as an intercultural educator which implies affiliation with an education department or school. If they are among the readers, it is their responsibility to augment, modify or refute what is presented here.

Terminology

There is little difficulty defining education. It is ". . .the process by which a culture introduces its members to the skills, attitudes, information, knowledge and values that will make it possible to preserve and enhance the culture" (Walsh, 1973, p. 10). It is through some form of education that we become a part of our culture. Responsibility for this education varies with the culture; it may be the parents, the school, the church, the government, or a combination of these. To this definition we might add that education is a lifelong process of growth in intellectual and emotional competency that enables people to cope with human existence both as individuals and as members of groups (Pusch, 1979, p. 4). To become *intercultural*, the education process must first analyze one's own culture—its precepts, value orientations, and patterns of thinking. An understanding of these facets will then be used as a basis for determining how best to interact with people in another culture. This last process is the focus of *intercultural communication*.

The difficulty arises in sorting out the overlapping terms: transcultural, intercultural, crosscultural, global, and multicultural education. All have been used to refer to the education described above. We can find a common core of concern for knowledge, *per se*, but why should there be so many terms? The *Thesaurus of ERIC Descriptors* (10th edition, 1984) offers its own nomenclature. A researcher investigating intercultural education is referred to multicultural education; this scriptor has been indexed since January, 1979, with 354 CIJE citings and 864 RIE; and "global approach" (including the subheading *education*) lists respectively 712 and 918 entries since October, 1974. Crosscultural education, however, shows 1,361 and 1,525 entries since August, 1969. This heading includes cultural education. Interestingly enough, the term crosscultural communication is not indexed; instead the user is referred to intercultural communication which has been included for less than three years. All indications are that a less than mutually accepted systematic use of terms exists. Hoopes and Pusch devote an introductory chapter to definitions choosing *multicultural*.To some extent, the term *multicultural* seems to focus on ethnic aspects, but it is true mainly in education-oriented materials. Given the following definitions from Hoopes and Pusch, it is difficult to understand either their distinction or basis for preference:

Multicultural education is a structured process designed to foster understanding, acceptance, and constructive relations among people of many different cultures. . .[It] is *not* just a set of ethnic or other area study programs but an effort to demonstrate the significance of similarities and differences among culture groups and between individuals within those groups.

Intercultural (crosscultural) education is educational activity which fosters an understanding of the nature of culture, which helps the student develop skills in intercultural communication and which aids the student to view the world from perspectives other than one's own (Pusch, 1979, pp. 4-6).

If they are both types of education, they are both processes, not just activities, and neither is limited to an ethnic focus. *Multicultural* education should be as concerned as *intercultural* with developing communication skills, which do not belong solely to either. The situation is reminiscent of the conversation in Lewis Carroll's *Through the Looking Glass* when Humpty Dumpty says to Alice, "Words mean what I choose them to mean." To this writer, the prefix *inter* is more descriptive of the desired process goals listed in both definitions quoted than is *multi*. What is important is the relationship implied by *inter*: "among, mutual, reciprocal," rather than the quantity of cultures involved (McKechnie, 1979, p. 955). For this reason, intercultural education will be used for the remainder of this chapter.

Interest in how people of another culture interpret the life of man and the nature of things has arisen in several disciplines during the last fifty years. Each has chosen terminology and formulated stipulative definitions. And there has been considerable borrowing, just as cultural anthropology borrowed from linguistics to create the terms "emic" and "etic." A pragmatic attitude has prevailed with emphasis on usable knowledge, and allowed scant concern for attention to theory as models or any other form. As a result, there is little theory, a proliferation of terms, and even less uniformity in their intended meaning.

Historical Perspective

Intercultural education (or whatever term is used to describe that learning) has not gained wide acceptance. Perhaps it is because that type of education has been seen as a biproduct of learning in the real and fictional worlds. Surely what Marco Polo learned about how to deal with people in cultures new to him could be called an intercultural education. Alexis de Tocqueville's incisive comments about American life in the eighteenth century could be a chapter on North American value orientations in an intercultural test today. In literature, Odysseus' travails in the strange cultures he encounters makes Homer's *Odyssey* a seventeen year intercultural experience. Lastly, the hypothetical-culture approach used by Swift in *Gulliver's Travels* and by Orwell in *1984* focuses wholly on our relation to self and society. But somehow intercultural education as an entity did not emerge until recently. We all agree that intercultural learning takes place and has taken place since the beginning of time; as a recurrent theme in history and literature its existence cannot be disputed, but it has received scant attention as a subject worthy of teaching in its own right.

The aftermath of World War II saw the beginning of what Wendell Willkie forecast as *One World* (Willkie, 1943). We realized that we were interdependent as nation-states and as people. The advent of better communication linkage gave rise to the global village concept. The realization that others starve as we worry about weight control will no doubt produce yet another catch phrase to capture the spirit of mutual understanding and sharing. In spite of the confusion over terminology, our mutually shared goal is the nurturing of non-ethnocentric people with a desire to understand their brothers and sisters in other cultures. It matters not by what name they are known, Walsh's "universal person" (Walsh, 1973), Adler's "multicultural individual" (Adler, 1974), or Gudykunst and Kim's "intercultural person."

In becoming intercultural, we rise above the hidden grips of culture and discover that there are many ways to be "good," "true," and "beautiful." In this process, we acquire a greater capacity to overcome cultural parochialism and develop a wider circle of identification, approaching the limit of many cultures and ultimately of humanity itself. The process of becoming intercultural. . .is like climbing a high mountain. As we reach the mountaintop, we see that all paths below ultimately lead to the same summit and that each path presents a unique scenery. (Gudykunst and Kim, 1984, p. 232).

So in 1985 we find endorsement of the goal, but diffuse efforts toward realization. In U.S. colleges and universities, Communication Departments have introduced intercultural communication courses that encompass many of the goals of intercultural education. Had these been a part of existing Education Department courses or a part of active school curricula, the scope of intercultural communication might be more restricted today. Those of us teaching intercultural communication have little or no contact with our colleagues in Education Departments.

Notable Contributions

One of the most valuable aspects of preparing a chapter of this type is the vast amount of material that is reviewed. Several of the more notable contributions to the literature have been selected for brief discussion. Moving chronologically, the first is *Intercultural Education in the American School* by William Vickery and Stewart Cole in 1943. Written during World War II, it was a direct attempt to help the schools deal constructively with problems of intercultural and interracial tension at that time. They saw that intercultural education was concerned with behavior directly related to racial, religious, ethnic and socio-economic group conflicts in which the teacher had the responsibility to know and interpret new findings (Vickery and Cole, 1943, p. 148). They cited as persistent and difficult the task of determining what U.S. cultural patterns actually are and how they influence behavior. Ethnic differences were treated as one of several components within a cultural approach to American education, and were considered channels for favorable cultural interaction. The authors outlined a plan for a program of intercultural education from primary grades through senior high school. Their contribution is notable for its position that intercultural education should permeate the whole of the American education system rather than be added to any one subject or sequential grouping of grades. How surprised and disappointed they would be to see that forty years later this planning has remained "on the drawing board."

Most provocative of the older books is John Walsh's *Intercultural Education in the Community of Man* (1973). It was one of the first full treatments of the subject from a theoretical standpoint. Unfortunately, it does not seem to have had an impact on education circles, nor was it discussed in communication literature. It was scarcely reviewed, and then only in library journals where it was criticized for its somewhat repetitious, "pontifical" quality (Bach, 1973). Nevertheless, the content and thoroughness of treatment are unparalleled. Walsh's thesis is that contemporary people must revise their educational experiences and institutions to foster a knowledge of two cultures, one's own and a universal one drawn from a study of languages, literature and institutions (Walsh, 1973). Intercultural education, as he saw it, is as vast as "anything that contributes in any way to one's better and fuller understanding of another culture." He wanted individuals to know what another culture thinks and why it thinks that way. He also made an interesting distinction between understanding a culture and being understanding of another culture. By the former he means grasping intellectually the concepts above; by the latter he means openness, receptivity, and sensitivity to those values, but not necessarily commitment.

A more recent addition to the literature is *Multicultural Education: A Cross Cultural Training Approach* (Pusch, 1979). Despite the title, the book is the best source of information available in the field of intercultural education. It contains chapters on concepts and historical development as well as on curriculum and teaching strategies. This writer would prefer to see the term *education* used instead of *training* which traditionally has meant short-term, intensive, culture-specific sessions with a pre-selected group. Nevertheless, the focus of the book is on central education concerns, and it is indeed more than a manual. Its stated purpose is to provide background, resources and techniques for preparing teachers—and for their faculty. Its approach is multicultural, with "The Case of the United States" forming a subsection of a chapter on the historical development of multicultural education (Pusch, 1979, pp. 39-61). But, in the following chapter on curriculum, the assumptions are western, that is, the curriculum selections fit the U.S. education pattern, grade by grade. How useful are they to educators functioning in other than western settings? However, the book is a beginning; if the 1981 second printing means that the book is in demand, that is an excellent omen; we need more contributions like this.

Guidelines from Practitioners

A number of worthwhile articles by practicing education professionals are worthy of comment. In Bancroft's (1975) "Teacher Education for the Multicultural Reality," which appears in a Wolfgang's book of readings, *Education of Immigrant Students*, four propositions emerge that are important for teachers dealing with intercultural concepts in multicultural classes. We may summarize the discussion as follows:

1) Teachers need to realize significant differences in concepts that surface in class; for example, that work and play are not of equal value in some cultures. Thus, students (and their parents) may react adversely to school apportionment.

2) Teachers need to be attuned to markedly different world views that affect interaction on a daily basis. He uses two dialogues to show cultural differences in extending invitations.

3) Teachers have little experience analyzing their own culture and therefore lack experience to analyze other cultures.

4) Teachers need to overcome their ethnocentricity.

New ideas? Not really, but the information is oriented toward teacher awareness of the multicultural reality with which they must deal.

Lastly, two outstanding articles that deal specifically with understanding in the context of their learning milieu deserve mention. One is by Deena Levine (1982), appearing in Samovar and Porter's reader, and concerns the contrast between Saudi Arabian and Algerian ESL (English as a Second Language) students. The culture specific information, perceptions and conclusions make it a model for the kind of teacher training instruction that is essential.

Janis Anderson's (1985) "Educational Assumptions Highlighted from a Cross-Cultural Comparison" stresses the pervasive cultural influences reflected in classroom activity. She also explains how expectations of a proper learning environment are linked to one's own experience such that education is "a cultural dictate rather than a universal mandate." In general, she argues for deeper appreciation of other educational systems on the part of teachers.

A word must be added about three other significant contributions; two are books of readings and the third is a collection called *Culturgrams. Beyond Experience* is a book published by the Experiment in International Living; it offers educators a wide variety of exercises based—as is their philosophy—on a pragmatic approach, learning how to build bridges of understanding between people. *Toward Internationalism* is published by Newbury House; it provides readings useful to teachers in all nations who wish a deeper understanding of the components operating in intercultural communication processes. And finally, Brigham Young University's extensive series of *Culturgrams* and other area studies publications must not be overlooked. They have introduced thousands of people to new nation-states with brief but insightful material.

Some Suggestions

Among the strongest influences in shaping an intercultural person is mass media. With the spread of telecommunication systems, virtually no place is isolated. While expense and technological problems may limit the use of television in remote areas, radio continues to provide inexpensive and extensive coverage; its importance should not be overlooked. In developing countries with educational radio programming, illiteracy ceases to be a barrier to intercultural understanding. Radio listening is the first step beyond the confines of the group to which one belongs and from which one gains information. Even one transistor radio in a small village can provide new horizons in dealing with technical and community problems. As Dodd pointed out, this type of media exposure stimulates further exposure (Dodd, 1982, p. 253). He has included in his chapter on mass media an excellent section on its relationship to culture, and has developed a linear/nonlinear model to show how mass media functions in cultures (Dodd, 1982, pp. 257-9).

Films are another source of intercultural learning that is largely untapped. During the past few years many U.S. produced films have dealt directly with intercultural themes. Winter 1984-5 brought E.M. Forester's *Passage to India*; *Witness*, a film on Amish culture; and *The Gods Must Be Crazy* , an African tribal encounter with the twentieth century in which a Coca-Cola bottle plays the villain. *The Chosen* and *Gandhi* also contributed to our education. These films play to large and appreciative audiences, yet no attempt has been made to explore the intercultural themes outside the movie theatre. Why not develop a cinema group discussion series similar to that offered by the Foreign Policy Association's *Great Decisions*? This yearly set of eight sessions presents structured group discussions focused on specific topics accompanied by specially prepared reading material. It has been well received in the U.S. True, the *Great Decisions'* audience is self-selected, literate, and middle class; films attract a broader population. People enjoy discussing what they have seen. Whereas Walsh's idea was to draw from assigned literature (Walsh, 1973), the film suggestion requires less background, commitment, and preparation.

A third suggestion concerns culture shock. For those going abroad (for education, business or pleasure) and for those coming to our shores, the frustration that accompanies the chronological stages of a sojourn in an unfamiliar culture needs *full* explanation in terms of psychological and physical factors. That it can be a valuable learning experience is often overlooked. If culture-shock were treated not as short-term training or orientation but as *education*, we could teach it—from physical aspects of jet lag to coping strategies in social environments. We could also teach about reentry, especially to students returning from study abroad programs; they often feel discouraged and alienated upon return.

Initially, when this chapter was suggested to the writer, the theme was how to educate people toward intercultural education in the future. We are not ready for that. Until we have sorted out our diverse terms, and until we have begun to work together with education professionals rather than independently, plotting such a course is premature. We need to examine what has been written, tried and proposed. Then we must research techniques that have not been fully explored. We have a mutual goal but that is not enough. Having a mutual goal will not enable us to climb the mountain.

References

Adler, Peter S. "Beyond Cultural Identity: Reflections on Cultural and Multicultural Man." *Topics in Learning*. (August, 1974). pp. 23-40.

Andersen, Janis F. "Educational Assumptions Highlighted from a Cross-Cultural Comparison." L. Samovar and R. Porter. *Intercultural Communication: A Reader*. 4th ed. Belmont, CA: Wadsworth. 1985.

Bach, B.C. "Intercultural Education." *Library Journal,* 98 (November, 1973). p. 3261.

Bancroft, George. "Teacher Education for the Multicultural Reality." *Education of Immigrant Students*. Ed. A. Wolfgang. Toronto: Ontario Institute of Studies in Education. 1975.

Batchelder, Donald and Warner, Elizabeth G., eds. *Beyond Experience*. Brattleboro, VT: The Experiment Press. 1977.

Dodd, Carley. *Dynamics of Intercultural Communication*. 2nd ed. Dubuque, IA: Wm. C. Brown. 1987.

Gudykunst, William and Kim, Young Yun. *Communicating with Strangers*. Reading, MA: Addison-Wesley. 1984.

Levine, Deena. "The Educational Backgrounds of Saudi Arabian and Algerian Students." L. Samovar and R. Porter. *Intercultural Communication: A Reader,* 3rd ed. Belmont, CA: Wadsworth. 1982.

Pusch, Margaret D., ed. *Multicultural Education: A Cross Cultural Training Approach.* Chicago, IL: Intercultural Network. 1979.

Smith, Elise C. and Luce, Louise F. *Toward Internationalism.* Rowley, MA: Newbury House. 1979.

Tyler, V. Lynn, ed. *Culturgrams.* Provo, UT: Brigham Young University, David M. Kennedy Center for International Studies. 1986.

Vickery, William and Stewart, Cole. *Intercultural Education in the American School.* New York, NY: Harper. 1943.

Walsh, John E. *Intercultural Education in the Community of Man.* Honolulu, HI: University Press. 1973.

Webster's Unabridged Dictionary, 2nd ed. McKechie, Jean, ed. New York, NY: Simon and Schuster. 1979.

Willkie, Wendell. *One World.* New York, NY: Pocket Books. 1943.

Educational Exchange in Europe: Trends and Challenges for Intercultural Learning
Roberto Ruffino, Ph.D.

There is an enormous quantity of activity going on in the field of intercultural exchange throughout the world. This mere transfer of bodies from one geographical area to another may have results, but intercultural learning is not one of them. For instance, in 1978, after a long period of dictatorship, Greece went back to a more democratic form of government and, as a result, was admitted to the European Community. In this process, Greece participated in a number of international activities to promote its international image, which had deteriorated severely.

One of the activities was a gigantic meeting of one thousand European and Greek young people, age 18-19, in Greece for two weeks during the summer. They lived together and discussed the role of Greece in the past and the present, and its future integration within European institutions. Each European country was responsible for the selection of fifty young people to send to Greece. Most of them did, but forgot about the whole issue afterwards. England has an institution which is called the Central Bureau for International Visitors and Exchanges. This bureau not only selected the participants and took them to Greece, but followed up with a questionnaire immediately after they returned back home, six months later and one year later. They wanted to research the British impression of this exposure to nineteen other European nationalities, and more specifically to the Greek group, the predominant group at the meeting. What was interesting is that one year after the return home almost all of the fifty British youths were in correspondence among themselves. Not one of them was in correspondence with a foreigner, least of all with a Greek. Before going, these fifty young people were strangers; one year later, they were still very close friends.

This is one of the instances where the international exposure served as a common enemy to bind a group together. Indeed the result of the experience was not intercultural learning. It was monocultural learning. It was bringing a group together rather than opening it up to outsiders. This result is happening much more often than we anticipate; we just do not have research to demonstrate it. Some field research by the Franco-German Youth Office, which was established in 1963, has samples of the results of exchanges. However, we lack systematic long range research on intercultural exchange. I believe that a large number of youth exchanges within Europe, between Europe and the United States, or in other world areas are indeed the transfer of bodies which reinforces national identities—local cultural identities—rather than helping people to open up to intercultural communication. The promotion of intercultural learning through youth exchanges is an immensely important consideration. Intercultural learning taps theory and practice in education communication, cultural anthropology, psychology, interpersonal relationships, sociology, economics, history, and the role of religion.

One of the main sources of misunderstanding is the inability to comprehend the meaning of the new symbols in the new culture or the easiness with which one misinterprets the symbols which may look the same as in one's own culture but have a different meaning. The role of class differences within a given society is one of the most difficult things for an outsider to perceive. For instance, it took me 20 years before I realized the role of class differences within the United States; not the visible differences that are associated with racial divisions, but class differences within the white U.S. society stemming from speech, education and occupation. The history of institutions in a given country and the role of values and behaviors remind us of the importance of a number of considerations.

Factors Contributing
to Intercultural Learning

There are some basic prerequisites that a participant must have in order to approach educational exchanges with a desire to attain intercultural learning.

The Knowledge of Self

The knowledge of self means the knowledge of one's own roots and especially the knowledge of the peasant societies within one's own country, the knowledge of religious values and the vision that one's society has of the future. This is often disregarded. However, one has to compare pasts and visions of the future as well. A society that does not have a vision of its own future may already be a dying society. This stream of consciousness, as it goes from the past to the future, goes into one's own peasant roots, even in an urban environment, and moves on towards the vision that one's society or culture has of the future. This is the prerequisite that one must have when approaching another culture.

The Readiness to Love

The second prerequisite is a readiness to love. In our Western European educational system, we have never stressed the importance of love in knowledge. Love is something that belongs to the realm of family, friends, and out-of-school activities. Schools have nothing to do with love in the Western European societies. Love is not considered a key to any form of knowledge, but it needs to be a part of the system.

Acceptance of Ambiguity

The acceptance of ambiguity is also significant. One must not go abroad or to another situation with the intention of classifying things as black and white. Even in the long range, one must be able to live with the sense of ambiguity and accept the poetry as a form of knowledge itself. This is not as a form to transcend knowledge, but as a form to approach knowledge, which is something very different.

In most of our Western European societies we immediately have a major drawback in accepting our own roots, accepting love and accepting ambiguity as ways to approach knowledge. This drawback is the Cartesian approach that is still prevailing in most European thinking. This approach maintains that I exist because I think, or I think, therefore I exist. This relationship binds together existence and intellectual activity as one, and emphasizes this aspect of human activity over all the others. This indeed is a major drawback to approaching the field of intercultural learning.

Trends in European Youth Exchange

Some of the trends that have occurred in youth exchanges in Europe in the last 30 to 35 years are insightful. The motivations that were behind these youth exchanges are particularly intriguing.

Although these trends are discussed chronologically, most of them overlap still today. However, certain trends may be more visible in certain periods of time and less so in other periods.

Post World War II

The first youth exchanges right after the war, the period that begins in 1945, obviously were geared at promoting peace and understanding and, at the same time, at learning a skill. A skill may very well be a foreign language or perhaps a professional skill, i.e. something aimed at improving one's own professional assets in view of a future career. The first of the scholarship schemes after the war were mostly for university students, graduate students, or people that finished at least secondary schools and were trying to learn another language or skill in another country. By being part of an exchange, they were also getting to know other people in other parts of the world and thus, hopefully, overcoming this "war" feeling that had been strongly present for so many years. In this period, we basically see the continuation of a tradition that had already existed before the war; a colonial tradition by which the people from the South used to go and learn skills in the North. Even today there continues to be a stream of students coming from Africa or Asia to Europe, especially Paris and London, to take their courses in French and English universities.

Another characteristic of the time is that a new wave of exchanges began. This was geared towards the USA for the Western European countries, and towards the USSR for countries that had become allied with the Soviet Union after the war. These new trends originated as a result of the war: The Eastward trend to Moscow, the Westward trend to the United States, in addition to the old French and British trends originating from the colonial times.

Rediscovery of Heritage

A turning point in this situation came around 1963 when a movement began which I call SOS, meaning the Search for Our Souls. It is the beginning of the "Hippie Movement" in the United States and Europe. It was the beginning of the refusal of the West as a source of wisdom, as a source of knowledge. Those in this movement no longer looked Eastward toward the socialist countries, but looked Eastward towards Asia as the source of wisdom. It was a time when throngs of young people from Europe travelled to the East, to India as a source of knowledge that had been forgotten. It was the dream of bringing somehow back together, if they ever were together, the East and the West—our Indo-European world. All the languages in Europe, with very few exceptions, are Indo-European languages, but the Indo side of the language or the culture has been put down for many centuries. The youth movement, which began in 1963, tried to rediscover this heritage and bring it back into the picture.

Helsinki Period

Another turning point comes in 1975, the year the Helsinki Act was signed. The Helsinki Act was the first agreement involving all of the Eastern and Western European countries to promote better communication, at least, between the two blocs in Europe. This marked the beginning of the new wave of attempts at starting educational activities that involved youth of the two parts of Europe.

One reason for the failure to develop exchanges between the East and the West is found not in the negative political climate as much as in the lack of *homology* between the two societies. By lack of *homology*, I mean that the society is set up in a way which does not have counterparts in the other half. In Western societies, exchanges are mostly based on private initiative from youth clubs or private associations which may start their own action independently of the government. In fact, in these countries, the government often does not even have an official bureau to deal with such an issue. However, in the Eastern societies everything in this field is handled through ministries and government offices. This very lack of homology means that when one country wants to start something between the two blocs, the individuals involved do not know with whom to dialogue. Eastern countries want to dialogue with a counterpart at their own level, and there is no such counterpart in the West. Most of the time Eastern countries are just not equipped mentally or bureaucratically to handle this kind of challenge because government bureaucracy follows very different patterns from private organizational bureaucracy. I have observed many attempts that failed, not really because of lack of political will on either side, but because of lack of ability to talk to one another.

This dialogue problem between East and West along with the problem of Cartesian thought are major problems in efforts to promote intercultural communication.

Search for Cultural Identities

Finally, I would mark another turning point around 1980: the beginning of the movement for cultural identities and cultural roots. It is the time of the booming of the ecological movement among young people. It is the time of the booming of the Third World movements which, in terms of youth mobility, means going from urban to rural societies; geographically means going from the new world, or the new worlds, towards the old worlds. An unprecedented movement not only from the United States to Europe but from places like Australia, New Zealand and many of the former colonies of Europe, and of Europeans towards Africa is seen. Many of the youth programs in Africa originate from the late 1970's or early 1980's. Africa carries many meanings to a European and offers one way of going back to one's own roots.

If these have been the trends in the course of the past forty years, what has been the attitudes of our governments and our institutions towards these demands that were coming from the youth in our countries?

Institutional Attitudes
Toward Youth Exchange

At the government level in most of the European countries, the reaction has been indifferent in most cases, or in the worst cases even counterproductive. By counterproductive, I mean action such as the ones that certain European countries have taken to protect their language in other parts of the world. This was of course sold to the general public as cultural exchanges or cultural action. For example, the French government invested an enormous amount of money not really to promote exchanges between Africa and other regions of the world, except Germany, but to boost up the cultural institutes around the world whose primary purpose was teaching French. This was done to stay competitive with English, which had become the most important language in the world. Still today, a number of countries have offices within the Ministry of Culture or the Ministry of Foreign Affairs, which call themselves cultural cooperation or cultural exchange offices. In fact these serve to maintain a network of institutions to teach their own national languages to other parts of the world.

There are three exceptions to this lack of interest in intercultural learning and intercultural communication through youth exchanges by the government.

First, the earliest exception began in 1948 in England. The English government established the Central Bureau for Educational Visits and Exchanges, which to date is the largest and most important institution in Europe dealing with this field. It is a coordinating body that makes available all possible information to young British people who want to visit other countries as well as for foreigners who want to visit the United Kingdom. Most of the work is indeed just spreading information, but a limited amount of their work has also been concerned with the educational content of the exchanges and research on the results of the exchanges themselves.

The second exception began in 1963 and involved France and Germany. Adenauer and DeGaulle decided to initiate a reconciliation plan between the two countries beginning with youth. An enormous budget was provided for young Germans and French to visit the other country. This program involved individual exchanges, class exchanges, young workers' exchanges, professional exchanges, and sport exchanges of all kinds. To date, approximately eight million young French and Germans have been to the other country thanks to this program, which is normally referred to in the European scheme as OFAGE.

The third exception, initiated in 1983, is the positive response that the governments of France, the Republic of Germany, Italy and the United Kingdom gave to an invitation by the President of the United States to discuss youth exchanges at a Williamsburg summit. Out of that summit originated the idea that the exchanges among the seven most industrialized countries in the world should have a new boost and more money. After that, the President's Initiative on Youth Exchanges originated, but that program ended at the close of 1985.

Little has been done at the national government level. Much more has been organized at the level of international, intergovernmental organizations in Europe beginning with UNESCO, which from its beginning in the late 1940's set up a system of associated schools that now extends to some 1,600 schools all over the world. Many schools are kept together in a world network and are encouraged to offer international curricula, exchange material among themselves and now, in the more recent years, also exchange pupils and teachers. It is the only network worldwide that allows for a number of East-West exchanges to happen. Otherwise, without the UNESCO umbrella, these exchanges would not be possible.

The Council of Europe also has been involved with this field. (Non-Europeans tend to have difficulty with these terms. The Council of Europe has nothing to do with the European communities. The Council of Europe is a body of 21 nations founded in 1949 dealing mostly with social and legal matters to try to bring Western European countries closer together. It has no influence on the economics, industry or agriculture of these countries.) The Council of Europe has established a program for the intercultural training of teachers, which is the only such program existing to date in Europe. There are 10 million displaced Europeans in Europe because of the economic situations. There are people who have to migrate from one country to another to find jobs. Therefore, new classroom conditions were created for students from six to eight different nationalities. In some European situations this is really extreme. The extreme case is in London where in an elementary school two years ago there were pupils of 121 nationalities coming from the Commonwealth countries, from some other parts of Europe, and some other parts of the world. Multiculturalism in the classroom is becoming such a reality that the Council of Europe has tried to tackle it in some way. One solution was to prepare material for the teachers to use in the classroom so that cultural diversity could be used as a richness. Hopefully, the quality of the work could be improved in the classroom and multicultural curricula could result in being an asset rather than a drawback to the teachers, who, otherwise, follow the traditional program set up for the class.

The Council of Europe has also set up two bodies in Strasbourg, the European Youth Center and the European Youth Foundation, with the specific purpose of financing international youth meetings in Europe. Youth organizations in different countries that are doing similar work and wish to meet face the high cost of travel. These institutions provide funds to allow youth organizations from different countries to hold meetings.

The European Community has also invested a considerable amount of money in youth exchanges, especially at the level of developing nations. There is an entire directorate dealing with the relationship between the 12 European countries and some other 65 countries in Africa, the Caribbean and the Pacific. There are cultural exchange programs with people of those countries. While the Economic Community involves only 12 countries and was established in 1957, it has much greater actions, much greater power, and a much greater budget to produce exactly what it aims to in the economic field.

Finally, the largest government investment in this field has been done at the level of local government. It has been at the county level in England, at the state level in Germany and at the regional government level in Italy that funds have been invested and opportunities have been created for exchange. In addition, there are the more private organizations like Intercultura, with which I am working, and others working on this area. Some of them originated as branches of U.S. based organizations such as Youth for Understanding or the Experiment for International Living, which now have European branch offices. Others originated as European institutions, but do not exist to the extent that they exist in the U.S.A. (although the phenomenon is still limited). Furthermore, in the framework of large national organizations, like political youth organizations such as the Young Socialist, the Young Christian Democrats or the Young Liberals, there is an office or a group that is dealing with youth exchanges.

Organizational Methodology for Youth Exchange

If this is the panorama of the situation in Europe, what are the methodologies that these organizations are following? Unfortunately, little thought has been given to methodologies.

A large number of institutions, for instance, simply expound the virtue of living in an international community. No real pattern is established. Not even in our sophisticated institutions, like the United World College, is there any course in intercultural learning. They just hope that by living together people will learn from one another in some way. Maybe through such a long exposure it happens.

Some other institutions believe that the only appropriate methodology is to put someone in a family and then leave him or her alone. The belief is that the family itself, being a microcosm of society, will be able to convey the values of that society to the hosted person. This may or may not work. It depends on the degree of awareness that the host family has of its own society; it depends on the social class; and, it depends on the personalities involved.

Some other organizations tend to work through an approach of joint projects—joint classroom work. In other words, two groups in two different countries start working on the same project. At a certain stage of the project they get together for several weeks and compare notes and see how the approach has been different in the two countries. Here, there are a variety of results in the field of intercultural learning. Some of these projects concentrate so much on content of the project itself that there is not much broad intercultural learning going on. Still others concentrate more on the differences of the backgrounds, i.e. why did we work in a different way?

Additionally, there are organizations that mix the home living with an activity outside the home. It may be living with a family and going to school, or living in a family and working in a company. For example, the young worker's exchanges, which the European Community started in 1979, bring workers between the ages of 18 and 28 to live in another European Community country for periods ranging from one month to a year. In this way it is believed that the family provides the emotional background as well as an introduction to everyday life, while the company or the school provides an introduction to the structures of the host society.

Other programs that exist among Europeans concentrate on age. Basically, three categories of agerelated programs exist. The ones that concentrate on young participants below the age of 12 stress the immediate emotional contact that very young people may have between themselves before they reach the age when they rationalize and intellectualize everything that they do. Next, there are exchanges in the age range of 15 to 19, aimed mostly at secondary school students. A third group of programs focuses on people at university levels or at young worker's level, age 19 and beyond. There are also programs that stress similarities between sending and hosting situations and programs that tend to stress the need for a contrast between the two to ease the reflection upon oneself that happens in the course of this exchange.

Finally, some programs are very short, while other programs stress the value of an extended exposure to another country. A few years ago I did research for the European Community. In the survey

I asked, "Why are you staying four weeks instead of only two? Why are you staying only 2 weeks?"

The answer typically was "because if we stay longer than 10 to 12 days, we start having troubles." The basic philosophy was going to another country, but avoiding all kinds of problems.

Actually, without crisis we do not have intercultural learning. There is a substantial difference between going to another country and avoiding problems and going to another country and facing problems. Youths should prepare themselves for problems and be able to cope with them. Otherwise, they just have a loss of identity and a crisis that does not lead anywhere. Given this prerequisite, I assume that programs in Europe that do not prepare participants to confront crisis situations do not promote cultural learning.

The Future of Intercultural Learning

In surveying program participants and organizers in Europe, they most commonly viewed their major goal as promoting peace by promoting understanding among people of different cultures. Many of them explicitly referred back to the opening statement of the UNESCO by-laws that states that since wars begin in the minds of man, it is in the minds of man that the defense of peace must be built. Even in this field where skilled learning seemed to be the main priority, it was only towards the end of the 1970's that intercultural learning emerged as a declared goal. In 1975, the European Federation for Intercultural Learning was founded. It was in 1979 that this European federation met within the framework of the Council of Europe and organized a colloquium on youth mobility and education. This was the first occasion in Europe that this new terminology and these new concepts were launched on a larger international scale to the educational community of the continent.

So the aim remains, although under different labels, to promote peace, to promote understanding, to promote some kind of international citizenship. Here is a struggle against other drawbacks that are found on the European continent. European history and languages divide the continent. In most cultures a foreigner has traditionally been seen as an enemy, as a devil, as an evil element—never as a god or as an equal. The word *barbaros* in Greek meant foreigner in a derogatory way, and today still means barbarian, which clearly means different in a negative sense. In Italy 2,000 years ago, the concept of Roman citizen equaled free man. If you were not a Roman citizen you were not free; you were a second class citizen. Throughout the middle ages, being non-Christian meant being non-human. Of course, some of these concepts have changed, but European history emphasizes difference.

There are also other obstacles. One is the protectionism of European society and the rigidity of its school systems. There is a belief that no other country has anything to teach in the field of education and schooling. Another obstacle is the class divisions within European society. Anything that appears as equal opportunity for everyone remains, in many countries, an opportunity only for the people who have money and who belong to the upper brackets of society. A third obstacle is the hierarchy of languages in Europe. There are languages that are more equal than others. Europeans want to learn English first, then French, then German and then who cares. So there are countries that become the constant pole of attraction. The intercultural element is often shadowed by this element of learning a language in order to gain a skill, in order to improve one's profession, in order to have a better career and make more money, rather than a real trend in getting to know neighbors and comparing differences.

Overall, we need to understand that most European countries do not understand what intercultural learning really is. It is not acquiring some new tools in order to communicate with one's neighbors, but it is changing one's mind from the depth. It is a concept for which the Greeks had a very good word—*metanoya*—the changing of your mind, which is a word that in fact has never been very successful in our culture.

Clearly, there are obstacles and there are challenges ahead. As a continent, Europe is currently squeezed between the mountain of the new worlds on both sides: industrialization on one side and the colonial demands by the developing nations, which were former colonies, on the other side. As a continent, Europe is split between east and west, north and south. As a continent, there is not a shared vision of the future. It is high time that we take a new look at ourselves, that we may gain a new perspective as a transcendent society, accepting the fact that values are unsure, and becoming comfortable with our current ambiguity.

Our history can help us rediscover important values and help us avoid common pitfalls. The future may also be in Africa, which is at our door, and may open new visions for the future. Africa is for us the real frontier for educational exchanges. It is the real otherness from what we are. It is the border that we have to learn to cross, mentally. We have crossed it many times in the past, physically and politically. It is the land where intercultural learning for Europeans may really find a deeper meaning, where differences are really different, and where the layers of these differences are more visible than elsewhere.

In the future we hope that the many strings that have been behind the youth exchanges in the past forty years may be drawn together again in the search of a new form of education:

The string of peace, the string of development, the definition of cultural groups and identities which have nothing to do with nation-states, and the acceptance of change as a permanent state and with it, the acceptance of migrancy.

In doing so, we will reawaken waves of memories that have been forgotten and, like the dunes in the desert that move back and forth and uncover things that were covered for centuries, we will learn to approach the future within a new intercultural spirit.

Name Index

A

Adler, N. J. 70, 80, 126
Anderson, J. F. 129, 131
Austin, C. 15, 16, 70

B

Bach, B. C. 127, 131
Baier, V. E. 6, 7, 8, 12
Bancroft, G. 128, 131
Bennett, T. 8, 10
Berry, J. W. 29, 42
Betances, S. 10, 115
Bojer, J. 70, 80
Brannion, D. 17, 92
Brown, M. J. 73, 80
Bwatwa, J. 78, 80
Burn, I. 77, 80

C

Capean, R. 79
Childs, J. 101, 110
Cisneros, H. 16, 52, 85
Clajus, D. 102
Cobbs, P. 14, 18, 56
Coles, R. 63
Crandell, J. E. 31, 42

D

Diego, J. 53
Deitweiler, R. 26, 42
Dodd, C. H. 3, 6, 7, 8, 10,
  130, 131
Downie, R. D. 75, 80

E

Elizondo, V. 53
Erickson, E. 57, 74
Evans, P. 103, 110

F

Fanon, F. 106, 110
Flores, P. 25, 65
Fontaine, C. M. 80, 81
Foubert, J. 102
Foyle, M. F. 70, 81
Frank, F. 76, 81

G

Glenn, E. S. 39, 42
Grove, C. L. 6, 8, 11
Gudykunst, W. B. 4, 6, 7, 8,
126

H

Hall, E. 38, 42, 107, 110
Hammer, M. R. 6, 8, 11
Hofstede, G. 30, 42, 101,
  104, 108, 110
Hood, K. 6, 11
Hui, H. 6, 11
Humble, J. 107

J

Janssons, D. P. 71, 72, 76, 81
Jiminez, R. 14, 18, 45

K

Kealey, D. J. 6
Kelly, H. H. 4
Kennedy, J. 121
Kim, Y. Y. 4, 6, 7, 8, 11, 126
Kipling, R. 76
Kluckhohn, F. 30

L

Laurent, A. 101, 110
Levine, D. 129, 131
Lewin, K. 36, 42
Lipsidge, M. 79
Lloyd, P. 102

M

Martin, J. N. 79, 81
Mason, S. M. R. 74, 81
Meintel, D. 74, 81
Mezei, L. 30, 42
Misher, J. 78, 80
Montalvo, F. F. 13
Moore, L. A. 76, 81
Morrow, L. 78, 81

N

Nakane, C. 38, 42
Naisbett, J. 86

O

Opubor, A. E. 72, 81
Ouchi, B. 103, 111

P

Parsons, G. 74
Pusch, M.D. 124, 128, 132

R

Ratui, I. 99, 102
Rhinesmith, S. 102
Rohrlich, B. F. 18, 123
Ringenberg, R. 78, 80
Rojas, L. 33, 42
Roper, C. 8, 11
Ruben, B. 71
Ruffino, R. 102, 133

S

Swap, W. C. 31, 43

Simcox, D. E. 78, 81
Skinner, B. F. 25, 43
Smalley, W. A. 74-82
Stevens, J. 100
Stewart, C. 127, 132
Strodtbeck, F. 30

T

Tannenbaum, A. S. 26, 43
Thibaut, J. W. 4, 12
Torbiorn, I. 6, 8, 11
Triandis, H. C. 13-14, 23, 24, 25, 26, 33
Tucker, M. F. 6, 7, 8, 12
Tyler, V. L. 129, 132

U

Umalgo, B. 53
Useem, R. 74, 76

V

Vanderkleut, P. 102
Vickery, W. 127, 132

W

Walsh, J. E. 123, 127, 132
William, O. 103
Wilkie, W. 126, 132
Wilson, E. 76
Wirtz, S. 101
Wiseman, R. L. 6, 8, 11
Wold, H. 78, 80

Y

Young, W. 70, 71, 81

Z

Zimmerman, C. C. 76-82

Subject Index

A

Acculturation 15, 16, 33, 34, 46-49
Adolescence 74-76
Aggression 62-63
Alienation (see anomie)
Allocentric 36-37
Ambiguity 6, 135
Anomie 36, 37, 52f

B

Blake and Mouton Managerial Grid 107

C

Canadian International Development Agency (CIDA) 94
Cartesian Approach 135, 137
Cognitive Framework 26f
Collectivism 28f, 32-41
Communication Apprehension 8
Communication Effectiveness 4-10
Commission on Central America 90
Consulting 99-105
Control 8, 25
Council of Europe 140
Cross Cultural Psychology 23f, 27

Culture 3, 25, 27f, 47, 106, 116-122, 127f (see also specialized headings)
Cultural Anthroplogy 134
Cultural Differences 65-67, 106, 117f
Cultural Exchange 89-90
Cultural History 63, 136
Cultural Identity 67-69, 118-122
Cultural Synergy 4
Culture Dysphoria Syndrome 76
Culture Shock, 2, 92-94
Culturgrams 129

D

Development 17, 18, 19
Dogmatism 7, 8

E

Economics 134
Economic Community 141
Emic 125
Empathy 7
Etic 125
Ethnicity 14, 15, 16, 57-64, 106, 116-118
Ethnocentrism 6, 14, 15, 36-37, 129
Ethnotherapy 56-64

F

Families 72-76, 79
Fatalism 8, 25
Feedback 109

G

Gift Giving 97, 98

H

Helsinki Period 137
Hispanics 33f, 45-55, 86, 87, 90, 91 (see also Mexican American)
Homogeneity 137
Human Resource Management 104-105

I

Idiocentrics 36-37
Individualism 28-30, 32f, 41
Innovativeness 8
INSEAD 100
Interconnectedness 47
Intercultural Communication 3-4, 9, 18, 108-109, 124
Intercultural Communication Climate 4, 9
Intercultural Consulting 16
Intercultural Education 18, 123, 131, 133f, 143
Intercultural Effectiveness 3, 4-10
Intercultural Exchange 133-145
Intercultural Identity 138
Intercultural Management 106-110
Intercultural Person 176
Intercultural Research 13-14, 18
Intercultural Respect 86, 87
Intercultural Skills, 3, 4, 95-98
Intercultural Training 9-10, 13, 17, 24, 25, 128f
International Trade 87-90, 92, 95-98
Interpersonal Comfort 7
Interpersonal Orientation Scale 31

Interpersonal Relations 59-60
Interpersonal Systems 9-10, 13

J

Japan 95-98

M

Media 18, 115-122, 130
Mexican American (45-55 (see also Hispanic)
Model of Intercultural Skills 9
Motivation 8, 25, 27
Multiculturalism 13-15, 17, 19, 85-91, 107-110, 116-118, 124, 125-126
Multicultural Education 124f
Myth 49-55

N

Nonverbal Communication 96-98

O

Openness 7
Oppression 61-64
Organizational Development 106-109
Overseas Diplomacy 6, 7, 8

P

Performance Appraisal 108
Personal Control 8
Power Distance 30, 40-41
Powerlessness 104, 105
Protectionism 144
Psychological Moratorium 75
Psychiatric Symptoms 71

R

Rage 63
Re-entry 15-16, 70-80
Repatriation (see re-entry)
Role 74
Rurality 14

S

Self-concept 74-76
Self-esteem (see self-identity)
Self-identity 8, 15, 48f, 56-58,
    61-63, 72, 74-76, 118-122,
    134
Self-orientation 6
SIETAR International 101-103,
    105
Social Interest Scale 31
Stress 8, 71f (see also re-entry)

T

Task Behavior 5, 6, 26
Third Culture Kids (TCK's) 75
Tolerance 4, 6, 8
Training 9, 10, 13, 17, 24-25
    (see also Intercultural
    Training)
Transition (see re-entry)

U

UNESCO 101, 103, 139, 140,
    143
Urbanity (see Urbanization)
Urbanization 14, 46, 85-90

V

Values 78-79, 123
Virgen de Guadalupe 52-54

X

Xenophobia 76

Z

Zajonc 25, 44